Raniero Cantalamessa, O.F.M.Cap.

THE MYSTERY OF PENTECOST

Translated by Glen S. Davis

D1242665

A Liturgical Press Book

THE LITURGICAL PRESS
Collegeville, Minnesota

www.litpress.org

Cover design by Ann Blattner. Icon: *Pentecost,* School of Tzznes, Crete, 1662. Church of St. George of the Greeks, Venice.

2   3   4   5   6   7   8

Library of Congress Cataloging-in-Publication Data

Cantalamessa, Raniero.
    [Mistero di Pentecoste. English]
    The mystery of Pentecost / Raniero Cantalamessa ; translated by Glen S. Davis.
       p.   cm.
    Includes bibliographical references.
    ISBN 0-8146-2724-2 (alk. paper)
    1. Holy Spirit—Mediations.   2. Pentecost—Meditations.   I. Title.

BT121.2.C25313   2001
242'.38—dc21   00-042845

Contents

Preface

The four meditations published in this book were presented originally to the Papal Household and form part of the series entitled *The Mysteries of Christ in the Life of the Church*.

Pentecost and, more generally, the working of the Paraclete are considered here according to the particular understanding given them by Luke in Acts, John in his Gospel, and Paul in his letters. By putting together these different but complementary points of view, one obtains a "three-dimensional" image of the coming of the Spirit, an image particularly suitable for promoting catechesis and devotion in the year dedicated to the Spirit in preparation for the Grand Jubilee.

This short volume complements the ampler and more in-depth one the author has written in his recent commentary on the hymn *Veni, Creator,* entitled *The Song of the Spirit.*

Chapter I

"And They Began to Speak in Different Tongues"

The Lukan Pentecost and the Spirit of Unity

Pentecost is a christological mystery—that is, it pertains to Jesus Christ. In a passive sense—namely, in relation to the *one sent*—Pentecost is the coming of the Holy Spirit, the pneumatological mystery par excellence. But in an active sense—in relation to the *sender*—it is a mystery that pertains also to Christ. The apostle Peter explains the event of Pentecost in this way: "Exalted at the right hand of God, he received the promise of the holy Spirit from the Father and poured it forth, as you [both] see and hear" (Acts 2:33). It is Christ who has poured forth the Holy Spirit! Moreover, Pentecost is a christological event also in a passive sense since the *one sent* on that day upon his disciples was none other than "the Spirit of Jesus," the "Spirit of the Son," the third person of the Trinity insofar as he was received and historicized in the man Jesus of Nazareth.

Above all, Pentecost is a christological mystery because of the reality of the mystical body. St. Paul says that, ascending to heaven, Christ "gave gifts to men" (Eph 4:7). But the verse of the Psalms that he cites here says rather the contrary—namely, that he "received gifts in men" (Ps 68:19).[1] Why this change of verbs? Both the former and the latter are true, explains St. Augustine. It is indeed the same Christ who gives and who receives the Holy Spirit: he gives the Holy Spirit insofar as he is the head; he receives it insofar as he is the body. "He gave to men, as the head to His members, and the self-same One received them in men, especially in his own members. . . . Christ Himself, therefore, both gave from heaven and received on earth."[2]

But why only now, at the end of the biblical revelation, is the third person of the Trinity made manifest to the world? Using the

1

concept of divine pedagogy, St. Gregory of Nazianzus gives this response, one that even today retains its validity. He writes,

> The Old Testament proclaimed the Father openly, and the Son more obscurely. The New Testament manifested the Son and suggested the Deity of the Spirit. Now the Spirit Himself dwells among us and supplies us with a clearer demonstration of Himself. For it was not safe, when the Godhead of the Father was not yet acknowledged, plainly to proclaim the Son; nor when that of the Son was not yet received to burden us further (if I may use so bold an expression) with the Holy Ghost.[3]

When it is said that "now the Spirit . . . supplies us with a clearer demonstration of himself," that "now" indicates the time of the Church, in which faith in the Holy Spirit reaches its zenith and the great torch that symbolizes the dogma of the divinity of the Holy Spirit is placed—as the same saint will say—on the candelabra of faith, the Creed.[4]

The explanation given by Gregory is also confirmed by looking at history. It was necessary that the Church first reach the certainty of the full divinity of Christ—which happened at the Council of Nicea in 325—in order that it might then reach the point where it could define also the divinity of the Holy Spirit, which took place soon after, a few decades later in the ecumenical Council of Constantinople in 381.

The discourse on the Holy Spirit presents another characteristic that pertains not so much to the *time* as to the *means* of knowing him. In speaking of God the Father we can base ourselves, in some measure, also on philosophy and theodicy (in fact, the so-called "God of the Philosophers" also exists!). In speaking of the Son, we can base ourselves on history, from the moment that he became flesh, and, indeed, it is by means of history that today we prefer to approach him. But in order to speak of the Holy Spirit what means do we have at our disposal? None. Only Scripture. Or, better put, we have, yes, one means and a great means, one that does not, however, belong to any human science. We have "spiritual" experience! Jesus himself indicated this means when he said of the Spirit that the world: "neither sees nor knows it. But you know it, because it remains with you, and will be in you" (John 14:17).

Our discourse on the Holy Spirit will be based, therefore, uniquely on these two foundations: Scripture and experience. By "experience" I do not mean only my personal experience or only the experience of human beings of today but also the experience of others and of the past—in other words, the tradition. The experience of the Spirit in the Church is nothing other than what we call the tradition of the Church.

A word on the spirit and interior attitude with which we make this rereading of the event of Pentecost. Of the sacraments one says in theology that "by signifying they cause"—that is, that they produce or realize that which they indicate with their signs. But one must also say something similar about the word of God. It too "by signifying or saying, causes"—that is, it realizes, makes exist, that which it expresses; it does not merely recount it. The clearest case of this is the consecration of the Eucharist. The Church through the mouth of the priest recounts what happened at the Last Supper: "On the night he was betrayed, he took bread. . . ." Through the explicit instruction of Christ himself, when this recounting of the institution is done in the proper manner by the proper persons, it brings about that which it tells. It is not limited to narrating what Jesus did then at the Last Supper but renders it actually present. In this strong way, the transformation is realized only through the Eucharist, through the presence of Christ in the Church; but on a different level it takes place also through the presence of the Holy Spirit.

Listening with faith to what was accomplished in the Upper Room fifty days after Easter, our task is not simply to recount or to hear. By its nature, by the nature of the word of God which is "alive and efficacious," it aims to renew, to make present, and operative again what was accomplished at that time. Since at that time it was written that "all were full of the Holy Spirit," in the same way now we must aim to be "all full of the Holy Spirit." This is the true purpose of our celebrating of Pentecost; it is not simply an historical but a "spiritual" purpose. It becomes spiritual not, to be sure, on account of the merit of the one who speaks or those who listen but uniquely through the grace of that God who wishes to give his Holy Spirit and seeks every occasion to be able to do so. For this reason, our entire reflection on the mystery of Pentecost will be accompanied, as if by uninterrupted background music, by the submerged plea that rises from the depth of the heart: *Veni Sancte Spiritus,* "Come, Holy Spirit."

1. *"For in One Spirit We Were All Baptized into One Body"*

The account of Pentecost in the Acts of the Apostles begins with the indication of the time and the place: "When the time for Pentecost was fulfilled, they were all in one place together" (Acts 2:1). Thus, the time is that in which the Hebrews celebrated the feast of Pentecost and the place is that of the Upper Room into which the apostles had retired after the Ascension of Jesus (cf. Acts 1:13). In the following verses the description of the miracle proceeds with rapid strokes from the external to the internal, from visible signs to spiritual reality. "The second verse tells objectively of a great noise that filled the house in which those assembled were staying; the third verse of the tongues [of fire] that appeared above each one of them; finally, the fourth verse of the real and proper effect indicated and carried out by these phenomena: *And all were filled up with the Holy Spirit.* This being filled with the Holy Spirit is expressed in the fact that they began to speak in other tongues."[5] The "new language" is a sign and a manifestation of the "new heart" that the Spirit has created in them. These men have broken the barrier of their own language, symbol of all the barriers that divide human beings from one another—the barriers of race, culture, sex, class, wealth, and the like.

At this point what had happened at the birth of Christ, which Luke describes at the beginning of his Gospel, is repeated. The event cannot remain hidden, the news of the incident overflows and is spread abroad. This time, however, it is not a question of a few Palestinian shepherds but of representatives of every nation under heaven, of which Luke even provides a list. The amazement reaches its peak when each person hears the apostles speaking his own tongue.

The exegetes agree in maintaining that by describing it in this way Luke wanted to emphasize "the universal mission of the Church" as a sign of a new unity among all peoples. This intention of Luke—and therefore of the Holy Spirit who inspired him in his writing—becomes more precise as we go forward in our

4

reading of Acts. The Spirit works in two ways for the humanity of the Church: on the one hand, he urges the Church outwards to embrace in its unity an ever greater number of categories and persons; on the other hand, he impels it inwards to consolidate the unity attained. He teaches it to extend itself in universality and to collect itself in unity.

We see the first of the two movements in progress in chapter 10 of Acts in the conversion of Cornelius. To what point must the universality of the community of the disciples of Christ extend itself and who is called to enter into it? After the experience of the day of Pentecost, the apostles were ready to reply: all the Jews and those observant of the Law, no matter what people they belonged to. In fact, such were those who on the day of Pentecost had adhered to the faith. But another Pentecost occurred, very similar to the first—and it occurred in the house of the pagan centurion Cornelius—to induce the apostles to widen the horizon and let fall the final barrier, that between Jew and Gentile.

The second movement we see in progress in chapter 15 of Acts during the council of Jerusalem where the problem is how to act so that the universality of the Church does not compromise its internal unity. In the course of the long and painstaking journey of the Church towards the pagans, the Holy Spirit reveals another of his ways of bringing about unity, a way that we must learn to recognize. He does not always work in the Church in a dramatic fashion, with miraculous interventions that resolve problems at once, as at Pentecost. He also and more often works in another mode, with a discreet presence and subtle activity, respecting the times and human differences, passing through persons and institutions, prayer and debate, orienting everything—even if over long stretches of time—towards carrying out the designs of the Father. In this way, in fact, he worked in the Council of Jerusalem as it addressed the question of the attitude to take towards the converts from paganism, the answer to which was announced to the entire Church with the words: "It is the decision of the Holy Spirit and of us . . . ." (Acts 15:28).

In the vision of Luke, therefore, the Spirit that came upon the apostles at Pentecost and that since then continues to guide the path of the Church in history is fundamentally a Spirit of unity. With one single phrase St. Paul takes up again this understanding of the role of the Spirit, an understanding he shared: "For in one Spirit we were all baptized into one body, whether Jews or Greeks . . . ." (1 Cor 12:13).

2. *The Holy Spirit, Soul of the Church*

The word "universal" originally means that which is turned towards the one *(uni-versum)*, that which aims at forming something unitary. Therefore, it does not indicate per se only a centrifugal movement towards the outside, but also a centripetal one towards the inside. The Church is universal not only when it aims to reach "the ends of the earth" but also when it tends towards its center which is the head of the body, the risen Christ. In this sense, universality and unity coincide and the Spirit of unity is also the Spirit of universality of the Church.

Over time the tradition of the Church has often seized on this meaning of Pentecost regarding the universality and unity of the Church. Explaining Pentecost, St. Irenaeus writes, "With one accord in all languages, they uttered praise to God, the Spirit bringing distant tribes to unity and offering to the Father the first fruits of all nations."[6] According to the more ancient explanation, Pentecost was the feast of Weeks when the priest in the temple offered to God the first fruits of the new harvest (cf. Lev 23:10). St. Irenaeus sees in this a figure realized in Christian Pentecost, when the Holy Spirit offered to the Father "the first fruits of all the nations" redeemed by Christ. The same saint tries to explain by means of an image how the Holy Spirit realizes this new unity. "Just as," he says, "dried wheat without moisture cannot become one dough or one loaf, so also we who are many cannot be made one in Christ Jesus without the water from heaven."[7]

St. Augustine, assailed as he was by the problem of the Donatists who cultivated a particularistic and sectarian idea of the Church, dedicated almost all his discourses on Pentecost to illustrating what it means for the unity of the Church. In one of them he writes, "So it is, that just as at that time the languages of all nations in one person indicated the presence of the Holy Spirit, in the same way he is now indicated by the love of the unity of all nations. . . . So then, the time you can be sure you have the Holy

Spirit is when you consent through sincere charity firmly to attach your minds to the unity."[8]

St. Augustine, too, like St. Irenaeus, has recourse to an image in order to explain this relation between the Holy Spirit and unity, the image of what the soul does in the human body. He writes, "In fact, what the soul is to the human body, the Holy Spirit is to the body of Christ, which is the Church. The Holy Spirit does in the whole Church what the soul does in all the parts of one body. But notice what you should beware of, see what you should notice, notice what you should be afraid of. It can happen in the human body—or rather from the body—that one part is cut off, a hand, a finger, a foot; does the soul follow the amputated part? When it was in the body, it was alive; cut off, it loses life. In the same way, too, Christian men and women are Catholic while they are alive in the body; cut off, they have become heretics; the Spirit does not follow the amputated part. So if you wish to be alive with the Holy Spirit, hold on to loving-kindness, love truthfulness, long for oneness, that you may attain to everlastingness."[9]

This famous image of the Holy Spirit as the soul of the Church helps us to understand something important. The Holy Spirit does not bring about the unity of the Church, so to speak, from outside, as only an efficient cause; he does not urge only towards unity nor does he restrict himself to commanding to be united. No, he "is" and "makes" unity. He himself is the "bond of unity," exactly as the soul is of the body. The expression so dear to the liturgy "in the unity of the Holy Spirit" means "in the unity *that is* the Holy Spirit."

This traditional reading of the account of Pentecost was, in fact, made by Vatican II, when it said: "On the day of Pentecost, however, he came down on the disciples that he might remain with them forever (see John 14:16); on that day the Church was openly displayed to the crowds and the spread of the Gospel among the nations, through preaching, was begun. Finally, on that day was foreshadowed the union of all peoples in the catholicity of the faith by means of the church of the New Alliance, a church which speaks every language, understands and embraces all tongues in charity, and thus overcomes the dispersion of Babel."[10]

3. *Pentecost and Babel*

But why, among the various phenomena that accompanied the coming of the Holy Spirit upon the apostles, does Luke give so much emphasis to the phenomenon of the tongues? Here it is not just a question of the well-known gift of speaking in unknown tongues during a prayer assembly. In practice, such speaking must always be followed by its interpretation on the part of someone else (cf. 1 Cor 14:27f.), whereas here there is no need for any interpretation because the miracle consists precisely in the fact that everyone understands immediately what the apostles are saying, as if each person had heard them speak in his or her own language.

The constant response of the tradition, maintained even today by the majority of exegetes, is that Luke wanted to create a tacit contrast between what happened in the construction of the tower of Babel and what takes place now in Pentecost. St. Cyril of Jerusalem, for example, writes: "In that former confusion of tongues there was a division of purpose, for the intention was impious; here there was a restoration and union of minds, since the object of their zeal was pious."[11] St. Augustine in his turn says, "Through proud men the languages were divided; through the humble apostles, they were reunified."[12]

This interpretation—common, as is evident, both in Eastern and Western Christianity—was welcomed into the liturgy, which inserted the episode of Babel among the readings for the vigil of Pentecost, and was maintained even by the initiators of the Reformation, Luther in particular.[13]

But what kind of relation really exists between the two events of Babel and of Pentecost? It is a question of an *antithetical parallelism*—one that contains both an element of affinity and one of contrast. The Church is the new Babel exactly as Christ is the new Adam. The element of affinity is that in both cases a project of unity among all peoples, made possible and manifested by the unity of language is at issue. There every people of the earth "spoke the same language" (Gen 11:1), here each person hears the apostles "speaking in his own language" (Acts 2:6).

The element of contrast consists in the type of unity pursued, and it is a radical contrast. The unity of Babel is a human unity, one decided by human beings and having for its aim the glory of human beings: "Come," they say, "let us build ourselves a city and a tower with its top in the sky, and so make a name for ourselves; otherwise we shall be scattered all over the earth" (Gen 11:4). "Let us make a name for ourselves!" not "Let us make a name for God!" It is a project of unity born out of the desire for power and fame, out of arrogance. At Pentecost, on the contrary, everyone understands the language of the apostles because they "hear them speaking in our own tongues of the mighty acts of God" (Acts 2:11). They are not raising a monument to themselves but to God. Stressing this element of contrast, one can rightly say that the Church is the anti-Babel rather than the new Babel.

The biblical teaching that springs from the pairing of Babel and Pentecost is thus that two types of unity are possible: a unity according to the flesh and one according to the spirit. The difference is the center. In other words, it is a question of knowing what is at the center of a certain unity, the point around which it is built, whether around God or around man.

Everyone wants unity. After the word "happiness," there is probably no other word that answers to such a compelling need of the human heart as the word "unity." We are "finite beings, capable of infinity" and this means that we are limited creatures who aspire to go beyond our limits in order to be "in some way all." We do not resign ourselves to being only what we are. It is something that makes up a part of the very structure of our being. Who does not remember some moment from youth (when these things are experienced for real and are understood much better than they are later on from books), who does not remember, I say, some moment of a consuming need for oneness, when he wished that the whole universe were enclosed into a single point and that he were, along with everyone else, in that single point? For this reason our sense of separation and solitude in the world makes us suffer. St. Thomas Aquinas explains all this when he says, "Since the one *(unum)* is a principle of being like the good *(bonum),* it follows that everyone naturally desires unity as he desires the good. For this reason, just as the love or desire of the good causes suffering, so also does the love or desire for unity."[14] This holds true primarily for the internal unity of every single person, but it is also valid for the greater unity with all other persons.

Someone has said that "hell is other people,"[15] and this affirmation can also be taken in a different sense than its author intended. The "others," those different from me, *are* that which I *am not*. And not so much because they *have* something that I do not have, as much as because they *are* something that I am not. Simply because they are. The simple fact that they exist reminds me that I am not everything. To be a particular individual, distinct and different from everyone else, means, in fact, to be that which I am and not to be all the rest that encompasses me. To be oneself entails the terrible consequence of not being other than oneself, a tiny isthmus of dry land or even a minuscule islet surrounded on all sides by the great ocean of my non-being. The others, then, are gulfs of non-being that yawn ominously all around me. From here to say that the others are my "hell," in a purely philosophical and, furthermore, atheistic vision, only requires one step.

The need for unity is the hunger for the fullness of being. We are made for unity because we are made for happiness. Unity or communion with others is, in fact, the only possible way to fill in those "gulfs" that open around us. At bottom, not only in matrimony, in which two persons unite to form one flesh, but also, in a different way, in the search for material goods and the search for knowledge, there is a need for unity, a need to annex as much "foreign territory" as we can.

How can we realize concretely this need for unity that exists more or less overtly in every rational creature? Here the roads diverge and the two projects of unity emerge: the unity of Babel and the unity of Pentecost—the unity according to the flesh and that according to the Spirit. In the unity of Babel everyone wishes "to make a name for himself," everyone places himself at the center of the world. Since we are so many and so diverse, on this road we can arrive only at "confusion"—as the very name "Babel" was from the first interpreted to mean. In this case, words only divide and the experience of the men of Babel comes to pass (even literally) who no longer understood one another and were separated.

Everybody wants unity, everybody desires it from the bottom of their hearts; however, it is so difficult to attain that even in the most successful marriages the moments of true and total oneness—not only of the flesh but also of the spirit—are rare enough and are, in fact, only moments. Why is this so? In general, it is because although we wish that there be unity, we wish it to be centered around our own point of view. This viewpoint seems to us so obvious, so reasonable, that we are astonished how other people do not agree and insist on their own point of view. We even sketch out in great detail to other people the road to take to get to where we are and to reach us at our center. The trouble is that the other who stands before me is doing the same thing that I am doing to him. So this form of unity only distances us from one another.

By contrast, in the unity of Pentecost or the unity according to the Spirit, one puts God at, or better accepts God as, the center. Only when everyone aims at this "One" do they approach and encounter one another. It's like the spokes of a wheel which near one another as they gradually proceed towards the hub until they join and form a single point. St. Thomas Aquinas calls the love of God "aggregative" and the love of self "disgregative." He writes, "The love of God is aggregative inasmuch as it brings human desire back from multiplicity to a single thing; self-love, on the other hand, disperses *(disgregat)* human desire in the multiplicity of things. In fact, a human being loves himself by desiring for themselves temporal goods that are many and diverse."[16] Thus, the love of God not only brings about unity among different people but also within one single person, an internal not just an external unity.

To pass from Babel to Pentecost signifies, to use an expression of Teilhard de Chardin, "to be decentered from ourselves and recentered on God."

The apostles themselves are the best demonstration of what we have just been saying. Before Pentecost when each one of them was seeking self-affirmation and personal supremacy and they took every occasion to debate "who among them was the greatest," nothing but petty disagreements and contests reigned among them (cf. Mark 9:34, 10:41). After Pentecost, when the coming of the Holy Spirit completely relocated the axis of their thoughts from themselves to God, behold, we see them forming a "community . . . of one heart and mind" (Acts 4:32) among themselves and with the other disciples. The new language that they learned and that everyone comprehends is the language of Christian humility.

It is this unity of the Spirit that must support and crown all the other unities, even the natural ones, of the believer: the unity of marriage, between man and woman, and the fraternal unity of the community. It is this unity that makes us exclaim with the psalm: "How good it is, how pleasant, / where the people dwell as one!" (Ps 133:1).

In the Spirit—that is, on the plane of grace—we can finally realize that need in us to be in some way the whole and not just scattered fragments of it. In this way, in the Spirit and thanks to the Spirit, the entire universe is gathered into a single point and I am in that point, happy to swim in the infinite ocean of the All that is God. Jesus had prayed precisely for this: "so that they may all be one, as you, Father, are in me and I in you, that they also may be in us" (John 17:21). And now, thanks to the Spirit, this prayer has come true. Everyone can "be one." "One body and one Spirit" (Eph 4:4): thanks to the Spirit we form a single body, we are no longer dispersed and fragmentary. "So we, though many, are one body in Christ and individually parts of one another" (Rom 12:5). Other people no longer are dark gulfs opening next to me but are part of me as I am of them. "We, though many, are one body . . . ." (1 Cor 10:17) and the same Spirit unifies us.

Look how a Father of the Church describes the unity among us and with God brought about by the Spirit: "Since we have received one and the same Holy Spirit, we are all, in a certain specific way, united, both to one another and with God. In fact, even if, taken separately, we are many and in each one of us Christ makes dwell the Spirit of the Father, nevertheless, the Spirit is one and indivisible. By means of his presence and his action he reunites in unity spirits that among themselves are distinct and separate. He makes of all, in himself, one and the same thing."[17]

Therefore, it is not the case that other people are my "hell." In a certain sense, they are my paradise because they permit me to be what alone I could never be without becoming God myself. We no longer need to look at one another with envy and suspicion. Whatever I do not have and others instead do have is also mine. You hear the Apostle list all those marvelous charisms and perhaps you become sad, thinking that you possess none of them. But, pay attention, St. Augustine admonishes you: "If you love, you do not have nothing; for if you love unity, whoever in it has anything has it also for you. Take away envy, and what I have is yours; let me take away envy, and what you have is mine."[18]

Augustine deduces this precisely from the fact that we are a single body. Only the eye of the body has the capacity to see. But does the eye perhaps see only for itself? Doesn't the entire body benefit from its capacity to see? Only the hand moves, but does it move only for itself? If a stone is about to strike the eye, does the hand rest tranquil and inert, saying that the blow is not directed at it? The same thing happens in the body of Christ: that which every member is and does, he is and does it for everyone!

The very sign of the tongues at Pentecost reminds us of this formidable secret. Even here, one could ask: Why is it that I have received the Holy Spirit and yet I do not speak any language as the apostles did? But in this way you too speak in every tongue as did the apostles. Are you a part of the single body of Christ? Do you love the unity of the Church? If so, then you speak every tongue since you make up a part of that body that speaks every language and in every language proclaims "the mighty acts of God." "Then, you see, each single believer was speaking in all languages; and now the unity of believers is speaking in all languages. And so even now all languages are ours, since we are members of the body in which they are to be found. . . . So it is, that just as at that time the languages of all nations in one person indicated the presence of the Holy Spirit, in the same way he is now indicated by the love of the unity of all nations."[19] Even today the most certain sign of the working presence of the Pentecostal Spirit in a Christian community is not speaking in tongues—glossolalia—but the love for unity, which is charity.

4. The Builders of Babel

Today perhaps we are in a position to discover in the juxtaposition of Babel and Pentecost something newer than what the Church Fathers discovered there. We are able to do so because the "spiritual" reading of the Bible increases and becomes richer with the progress of the historical knowledge that we have concerning the Bible. The "Spirit" grows as the "letter" grows because the former is founded on the latter.

Today we know something more precise about the nature of the enterprise narrated in Genesis 11, which the Fathers of the Church

13

did not know, and thus we can reap a new profundity from the juxtaposition made by Luke. Of what nature was the enterprise of Babel and who were its builders according to the Fathers? For them it represented a construction raised up "against the Lord" as a sign of defiance and proud arrogance. Its builders were "the giants," a species that corresponds in the Bible to the Titans who defy heaven in Greek mythology. "I mean, just as after the flood," writes St. Augustine, "the ungodly pride of men built a high tower against the Lord, and the human race was deservedly divided by languages, so that each nation would speak its own language and thus not be understood by the others; so in a similar way the devout humility of the faithful has brought to the unity of the Church the variety of their different languages."[20] In this light, the contrast between Pentecost and Babel coincides with that between believers and unbelievers, between the city of God and the city of Satan. The word of God smites the atheists, the blasphemers, those that rebel proudly against God.

Now all that is quite true, but there's more to the story. Today we know with relative certainty, thanks to the progress of historical and archaeological knowledge, that the project of building a tower that was raised towards the sky was not a project "against" God but, on the contrary, "for" God. In fact, the builders' intention was to build one of those multilevel towers (called *ziggurats*), whose various remains have been found in Mesopotamia and which served as "cult buildings of gigantic proportions."[21] The higher the edifice, the more they thought they could secure the benefits of the divinity.

What then was the "sin" of Babel and why did God confuse their tongues? The answer is contained in the same biblical story. Those men embarked on the enterprise saying: "Come, let us . . . make a name for ourselves . . . ." (Gen 11:4). They were not moved by genuine piety and reverence towards the divinity but by a strong will for self-affirmation, not by the quest for the glory of God but for their own glory and power. In this manner, God was turned into an instrument. To build a tower or a temple of unusual dimensions signified to proclaim their own power and ability to dialogue with the divinity as equals, so to speak, tacitly saying to him: "See what we were capable of doing for you? And you, what will you do now for us?" Babel is an episode of the eternal temptation of man to become God's creditor.

If this is the case, the sin of the men of Babel is not so much the sin of atheists but that of the pious and the religious, of those who know God but do not render him the glory and thanks due him. The sin punished by God in Genesis 11 is of the same kind as that denounced by Paul throughout his Letter to the Romans: the sin of wishing to save oneself by one's own powers, of reaching God by one's own works, of "winning" God, making of the things made for God—observance of the Law, performance of rites, acts of justice—an occasion for boasting.

The natural religiosity of man, that which he creates following his own sentiment, aims always at constructing some sort of high pyramid—made in some cases of intellectual and speculative powers and in others of ascetic works—at the vertex of which he thinks to reach God and dialogue with him. But the Bible has revealed to us something quite different. By becoming flesh, God has overturned the pyramid, has descended, has put himself at the bottom and supports all of us with his grace. Salvation lies in accepting the initial and fundamental gratuitousness of salvation. Here the way to go up is really the way to go down, as the philosopher Heraclitus once said. It is humility. "Not by an army, nor by might, but by my spirit, says the LORD of hosts" (Zech 4:6).

One understands now what the overturning brought about in Pentecost with the coming of the Holy Spirit consists in. In the heart of the apostles, God has taken the place of the I, has destroyed the vaunt of their works and their projects, and urges them to brag only of him, not of themselves. Augustine has seen rightly when he says that Babel is the city built on self-love, while Jerusalem—that is, the Church or the city of God—is the city built on the love of God.[22] The mystery of impiety has been turned upside down, the truth no longer held "prisoner of injustice" (cf. Rom 1:21ff.), man no longer puts himself in place of God, nor limits himself only to knowing God, but also renders him the glory and thanks due him.

The biggest surprise for me occurred when, through reflecting on who the builders of Babel could have been, I discovered unexpectedly and with overwhelming evidence that I—alas—was one of them. Biblical archaeology no longer was of use; a simple examination of conscience was necessary. It was not necessary to dig among the ruins of Mesopotamia to discover the remains of the tower of Babel; it was enough to dig inside myself. If we wish truly to take the final and decisive step towards the "truth," we must humbly recognize that the enterprise of Babel is still going on and that we are all—some more, some less—involved in it. The passage from Babel to Pentecost, which occurred historically once and for all and is narrated in Acts 2, must be carried out spiritually every day in our lives. We need to pass continually from Babel to Pentecost, as we must pass continually from the old man to the new man.

If the meaning of Babel were only the one brought to light, in their time, by the Fathers, it would judge, nowadays, only the non-believers, the atheists, or the proponents of a radically secular and "titanic" civilization. However, understood in this other way, the opposition Babel-Pentecost judges us also, the pious and religious as well—in fact, especially them. Whom do I resemble as I build my family, my community, the Church, as I act as a member of a pastoral council, as a priest, as a man of culture, as a writer or simple Christian—the builders of Babel or the men of Pentecost? In the end, it is easy to discover it. It suffices to answer the question: for whom do I do it? What is the final goal, the secret, of what I am trying to do? For whom am I trying to make a name— for myself or for God?

In a vision of the Shepherd of Hermas, the Church is likened to a tower: "The tower which thou seest building is myself, the Church. . . . Hear then why the tower is built upon water. It is because your life was saved and shall be saved by water. But the tower was founded by the word of the almighty and glorious Name, and it is held fast by the unseen power of the Master."[23] The Scriptures themselves liken the Church to a construction and a building (cf. Eph 2:21-22; 1 Pet 2:5). In the construction of this tower, destined truly to arrive "up to heaven," one can work in two ways and with two very different attitudes: either with the spirit of Babel or with that of Pentecost. The opposition between the two enterprises is thus truly in progress. We must convert ourselves, continually passing from one to the other. There are only two great open worksites in history and it is up to us to choose in which one to labor. The two accounts of Genesis 11 and Acts 2 also tell us the different end results of the two enterprises: on the one hand, confusion and dispersion; on the other, the wonderful harmony of hearts and voices; on the one hand, rivalry; on the other hand, unity.

St. Paul recommends that we "preserve the unity of the spirit through the bond of peace" (Eph 4:3). The unity of the Spirit must continually recreate and renew because the "disaggregative" forces of egoism and the action of the one whom the Scripture defines as "the devil," *diabolos,* he who divides, continually lay in wait to ensnare it. Just as unity is the prerogative of the Spirit of God, in the same way division is the characteristic of the satanic spirit. We must take the example of what the spider does with its web. If you examine a beautiful spider web outside above a hedge, you see how quickly the spider runs to restitch and repair every thread of its web as soon as a tear is produced in it (by whatever means) so that it always remains taut and whole in every part.

And what are we to do to renew unity every time it is threatened? St. Paul reveals to us the secret: "through the bond of peace." By reestablishing peace, by making peace. On the cross, Jesus reestablished unity—unity between Jews and gentiles, between God and the world—by making peace, and he made peace by destroying enmity in himself. Not by destroying the enemy, but by destroying enmity, which is another thing entirely. It is written:

> For he is our peace, he who made both one and broke down the
> dividing wall of enmity, through his flesh, abolishing the law with
> its commandments and legal claims, that he might create in him-
> self one new person in place of the two, thus establishing peace,
> and might reconcile both with God, in one body, through the
> cross, putting that enmity to death by it. . . . for through him we
> both have one access in one Spirit to the Father (Eph 2:14-18).

An episode from the life of St. Francis of Assisi comes back to my mind. As soon as he received the invitation of the Crucified— "Go, Francis, repair my house!"—he began to walk through the streets of Assisi, asking for stones to repair the little church of San Damiano and saying: "Whoever gives me one stone will have one reward; whoever gives me two stones, will have two rewards. . . ." We all have stones with us. We can put them to two different and opposed uses: either to throw them at our brothers in the form of judgments, reproofs, condemnations and excommunications, as the Pharisees were ready to do to the woman in the

Gospel taken in adultery (cf. John 8:3ff.) or to use them to build unity, either to destroy the enemy or to destroy enmity itself. Therefore it is now Jesus himself who addresses to us that invitation: "Whoever gives me one stone will have one reward; whoever gives me two stones will have two rewards; whoever gives me every stone will have every reward."

NOTES

1. All quotations from Scripture are from the New American Bible except this one. Here the NAB renders the phrase from the psalm quoted by the author as "received slaves as tribute." Since this version obscures the precise verbal echo of the psalm in Paul, an echo which Cantalamessa's Italian Bible preserves, the Douay version (Ps 67:19) which closely resembles it is quoted.
2. St. Augustine, *The Trinity,* trans. Stephen McKenna, C.S.S.R., *The Fathers of the Church,* vol. 45. (Washington, D.C.: The Catholic University Press, 1963) 499. [15.19.34]
3. St. Gregory Nazianzen, "On the Holy Spirit," *The Nicene and Post-Nicene Fathers,* Second Series, vol. 7, trans. Charles Gordon Browne and James Edward Swallow (Grand Rapids: Eerdmans, 1983) 326. [31.26]
4. Ibid., 247. [12.6]
5. Gerhard Schneider, *Gli Atti degli Apostoli* (Brescia, 1985) 336.
6. St. Irenaeus, "Against Heresies," *The Anti-Nicene Fathers,* vol. 1, ed. Alexander Roberts and James Donaldson (New York: Scribner's, 1908) 444. [3.17.1]
7. St. Irenaeus, "Against Heresies," *The Faith of the Early Fathers,* vol. 1, trans. W.A. Jurgens (Collegeville: The Liturgical Press, 1970) 92. [3.17.2]
8. St. Augustine, *Sermons, The Works of St. Augustine,* part III, vol. 7, trans. Edmund Hill, O.P. (New Rochelle, N.Y.: New City Press, 1993) 284–6. [269.3–4]
9. Ibid., 276. [267.4]
10. "Decree on the Church's Missionary Activity *(Ad Gentes divinitus),*" *Vatican Council II: The Basic Sixteen Documents,* ed. Austin Flannery, O.P. (Northport, N.Y.: Costello Publishing Co., 1996) 446. [n.4]
11. *The Works of St. Cyril of Jerusalem,* vol. 2, in *The Fathers of the Church,* vol. 64, trans. Leo McCauley, S.J. (Washington, D.C.: The Catholic University Press, 1970) 106–7. [Catechesis 17.17]

12. St. Augustine, *Enarrationes in psalmos*, in *Corpus Christianorum Latinorum*, vol. 39 (Turnhout, Belgium: Brepols, 1956) 665. [54.11]
13. Cf. Martin Luther, *Lectures on Genesis: Chapters 6–14*, vol. 2 of *Luther's Works*, ed. Jaroslav Pelikan (St. Louis: Concordia, 1960) 215 and passim.
14. St. Thomas Aquinas, *Summa Theologica* I-IIae, q. 26, a. 3.
15. Jean-Paul Sartre, *No Exit*, any edition.
16. St. Thomas Aquinas, *Summa Theologica*, II-IIae, q. 73, a.1, ad. 3. [ditto]
17. Cyril the Alexandrian, *Commentary on John* 11.11 (PG 74, p. 560). Trans. from the Italian.
18. St. Augustine, *Tractates on the Gospel of John 28–54*, vol. 3, *The Fathers of the Church*, vol. 78, trans. John W. Rettig (Washington, D.C.: The Catholic University Press, 1993) 48. [32.8]
19. St. Augustine, *Sermons, 284–5*. [269.1–2]
20. Ibid., 298. [271.1]
21. Gerhard von Rad, *Genesis: A Commentary*, trans. John Marks (Philadelphia: The Westminster Press, 1972) 150.
22. Cf. St. Augustine, *The City of God*, trans. R.W. Dyson (Cambridge: Cambridge University Press, 1998) 632. [XIV, 28]
23. *The Shepherd of Hermas*, *Early Church Classics*, vol. 1, trans. C. Taylor (London: Society for Promoting Christian Knowledge, 1903) 79–80. [*Visio* III, 3]

Chapter II

"You Will Receive Power When the Holy Spirit Comes upon You"

The Lukan Pentecost and the Spirit of Prophecy

Everything that Luke has previously narrated—the coming of the Spirit in the form of tongues of fire, the presence in Jerusalem of devout Jews of every nation, the astonishment of those present—should serve to lead the way for the speech of Peter which follows. In response to everyone's asking, "What does this mean?" Peter takes the floor and begins to speak in a loud voice (cf. Acts 2:12-14). This sequence of events reflects Luke's vision of the Holy Spirit and its function in the public debates of the Church. The other two Synoptics, Matthew and Mark, sticking closely to traditional pneumatology, present the Holy Spirit as "the divine power" that renders human beings—and now also Jesus of Nazareth—capable of performing marvels, actions superior to those normally possible for humans, such as casting out demons and combating and conquering Satan himself (cf. Matt 4:1, 12:28). This conception of the Spirit has a charismatic stamp, inherited from the Old Testament.

The novelty of Luke is that, of the various marvels and supernatural actions of the Spirit, he privileges one in the sharpest way: prophecy. The Spirit is the Spirit of prophecy; it is the power that makes possible speaking in the name of God and with the authority of God. In the life of Jesus, this is clear from the beginning. In the baptism at the Jordan, the Spirit came upon Jesus of Nazareth and "anointed him," above all, for one thing: "to bring glad tidings to the poor," in other words, to evangelize (cf. Luke 4:14-18).

What happened to Jesus at the beginning of his messianic activity is repeated in turn for the Church at the beginning of its mission. Pentecost stands to the Acts of the Apostles as the baptism of Jesus stands to the Gospels. His baptism was the Pentecost of Jesus; Pentecost was the baptism of the Church.

Later on in the book of Acts, Luke also illustrates this idea that the Holy Spirit is the gift of the Risen One to the Church so that it may be capable of bringing the good news to the world (cf. Acts 4:31). The Spirit's function is to proclaim the Word. It is already presented in this way, moreover, in Acts 1:8: "But you will receive power when the Holy Spirit comes upon you, and you will be my witnesses." Even the long quotation from Joel serves to bring to light that the Spirit, having descended upon the Church, is the Spirit of prophecy. Now, however, unlike in times past, this prophecy is extended to all the members of the new people, young and old, son and daughter, servant and slave.

We will understand better the peculiarity of Luke's vision when we will have had the chance to contrast it with that of John and Paul, in whom the Holy Spirit does not appear so much as a power and aid given for the mission of the Church as an internal principle that changes the heart and sustains the Church's very existence.

1. The Spirit and the Word

For Luke, therefore, the Holy Spirit is first of all the Spirit of prophecy. It is the power that guarantees the progress of the Word from Jerusalem all the way to the ends of the earth. From this starting point, let us set out to discover the relevance for our time of the narrative of Pentecost.

We need the Spirit of prophecy in order to bring, or bring back, human beings to God through the proclamation of the Gospel. In the book of Revelation, John says succinctly, "Witness to Jesus is the spirit of prophecy" (19:10). And this line recalls the "But you will receive power when the Holy Spirit comes upon you, and you will be my witnesses" of Acts 1:8. One cannot proclaim Jesus effectively except with the power of the Spirit. The apostles are "those who preached the good news to you [through] the Holy Spirit . . . ." (1 Pet 1:12). Between proclaiming Christ simply "in doctrine" and proclaiming him "in the Holy Spirit" there is the same difference as between proclaiming the word "from without," standing outside of its sphere of action, its dominion, and its "grip," free and neutral before it, and proclaiming it while standing "within" the word, in its mysterious grasp, moved by it, in vital contact with it, getting from it power and authority. In the first case there is a transmission of doctrine, in the second a transmission of existence.

St. Peter calls this speaking "with the words of God": "Whoever preaches, let it be with the words of God . . ." (1 Pet 4:11). In this case something is realized that recalls what took place in the moment in which the word was written down for the first time—namely, in biblical inspiration: "human beings moved by the holy Spirit spoke under the influence of God" (2 Pet 1:21). The day of Pentecost took place just this way. Moved by the Holy Spirit, those men spoke on behalf of God. And we know what happened: three thousand people felt cut to the heart and converted to the faith.

We need, I repeat, this prophetic mode of proclaiming the Gospel; otherwise, we would remain, despite everything, on the same level as the world. The content of the message will differ from every other proclamation—and this will already be a fundamental issue—but not the power or the principle that animates the message. "Is not my word like fire, says the LORD, / like a hammer shattering rocks?" (Jer 23:29). Surely it is, but "his" word, God's word! "His word" does not only mean the word "that speaks of God" but also the word "of the God that speaks," the word that has God for its subject not only its object.

The Bible speaks of a word "that comes forth from the mouth of the LORD" (Deut 8:3, Matt 4:4). It says that man lives "'by every word that comes forth from the mouth of God'" (Matt 4:4). Which is the word of which one can say that it issues from the mouth of God? What is the "living and effective" word (Heb 4:12)? It is *not* the word detached from God, taken from books, handled by people and proclaimed on their authority until it has lost any contact with its source. Living water is water taken directly from the spring, not bottled and shipped . . . And what guarantees this contact? What decides whether a word or discourse "lives" from God or not? It is, precisely, the Holy Spirit, the "breath" of God.

22

Let us start from human experience. Which word can I say is my "living" word? Surely, of none other than the one I pronounce out loud, the one that issues from my very own mouth, carried, articulated, and made resonant by my breath, that is propelled across the air to the ears of my listener by a puff of air from my mouth. And which word is God's word? That which is carried, driven forth, made resonant and effective by the breath of God which is the Holy Spirit! This is the primordial meaning of the expression "Spirit of God," especially in the prophets—the vital breath of God that animates and makes efficacious his word. The phrase "Spirit of God" implies the nearness of God to the word; God creates with the spirit or breath from his mouth—"By the LORD's word the heavens were made; / by the breath of his mouth all their host" (Ps 33:6).[1] This intimate link between God's word and his breath is attested in Isaiah, particularly in reference to the Messiah: "He shall strike the ruthless with the rod of his mouth, and with the breath of his lips he shall slay the wicked" (Isa 11:4).

In the New Testament this link between the divine breath and word flows into the mystery of the mutual relationship, or *perichoresis,* between the Word in person and the Holy Spirit, between the Son and the Spirit. Says Jesus, speaking of the Holy Spirit, "He will not speak on his own . . . he will take from what is mine and declare it to you" (John 16:13-14). "He will take from what is mine": what does Jesus have, what is his, if not the Word? The Holy Spirit, therefore, will take the word of Christ and will proclaim it. "He will not speak on his own": he will not add his words, new words, because everything that the Father had to say was through his word, and there are no more words of God after and outside of him. He will take from what is mine "and declare it to you." When I speak, the breath that is in me takes, so to speak, from my heart and my mind the idea or the innermost word formed or being formed there and carries it to whoever listens to me. The Holy Spirit does the same thing with the word formed in the bosom of the Father, Jesus.

Can my breath animate your word or your breath animate my word? No, my word can only be animated by my breath and your word by your breath. Thus, in an analogous way, the word of God can only be animated by the breath of God and the breath of God is the Holy Spirit! This is an extremely simple truth, almost obvious, and yet it has immense import. It is the fundamental law of every proclamation and every evangelization.

Between the two breaths or spirits—ours and God's—there is a metaphysically infinite difference, one that only biblical revelation has brought to light. The concept of *spirit,* understood as opposed to *matter* and as belonging to the dimension of eternity and as the "totally other," this concept so essential for our entire civilization, is a product of Christianity. Before Christianity, and in particular for the Stoics, between the two breaths, human and divine, there was only a difference of degree. According to them, even the Spirit was made of matter, matter "more refined" but always matter. "Even the Spirit is a body,"[2] one reads in the Stoic sources. Despite this lack, even the Stoic philosophers had intuited the vital link between the breath and the word, between *Pneuma* and *Logos.* Even for them, the "warm breath" of the *Pneuma* was a type of support and vehicle for the Word.[3]

One understands, then, the profound reason why one cannot proclaim the Gospel except "in the Holy Spirit." The Holy Spirit appears to us as the one who "gives voice to the word," as the one who "puts the word into the mouth" *(sermone ditans guttura),* as the hymn *Veni creator* sings. This is Luke's particular message, his specific contribution to the great revelation concerning the Holy Spirit. The Holy Spirit received in the Jordan confers power on the preaching of Jesus. When he speaks, "things always happen." The blind see, the lame walk, the sea calms, demons flee. When we read the story of the man possessed by an unclean spirit that cannot put up with the appearance of Jesus in the synagogue at Capernaum and begins to cry out "Have you come to destroy us?" it seems that we are present at the realization of the prophecy of Isaiah referred to above: "He shall strike the ruthless with the rod of his mouth, / and with the breath of his lips he shall slay the wicked" (Isa 11:4). The word of God is efficacious and energetic *(energes)* (cf. Heb 4:12, 1 Thess 2:13) because in it acts the spirit of God, divine energy, "power from on high."

In the Acts of the Apostles, Luke has presented some models; he has described how the Church began because its laws, its constants, and its perennial nature are held and made manifest in its beginnings. The apostles ask the Risen Jesus, "Lord, are you at this time going to restore the kingdom to Israel?" Jesus answers, "It is not for you to know the times or seasons that the Father has established by his own authority. But you will receive power when the holy Spirit comes upon you, and you will be my witnesses . . . ." (Acts 1:6-8). It is as if he had said: "Behold, how the kingdom of God comes. The Holy Spirit comes upon you, makes you capable of bearing witness to me, and this is the coming kingdom of God." Jesus says the same thing in the Gospel of John: "The Spirit of truth that proceeds from the Father, he will testify to me. And you also testify . . . ." (John 15:26-27). St. Peter expresses himself in the same way before the Sanhedrin: "We are witnesses of these things, as is the holy Spirit . . . ." (Acts 5:32).

At the time of the New Testament, an infinity of traditional religions and mystery cults populated the world. There were religious philosophies and itinerant preachers of Isis and other divinities. How was Christianity able to make its voice heard above such a din? How did it manage to attract so many people with such unalluring prospects as that of the cross and persecution? The answer is: the Holy Spirit!

Everyone recognizes that the Church had an experience of the Holy Spirit before it had a theology of the Holy Spirit, an experience linked to the baptismal liturgy, the cult, and martyrdom. It was this experience of the Spirit that led the Church towards the theology of the Holy Spirit and finally to the definition of his divinity. How can the Holy Spirit not be God if it sanctifies us and unites us to God? This was one of the principal arguments with which the Fathers arrived at the definition of the divinity of the Holy Spirit in the ecumenical Council of Constantinople of 381.[4] It contains some precious hints even for us. One rarely arrives at experience from theology, at the experience of the Holy Spirit from the study of the Holy Spirit. In trying to do so we run the risk of wishing to invert the relation with respect to what took place at the beginning, of starting from the *idea* of Spirit and never arriving at the *reality* of the Spirit, of reducing even the Spirit to ideology. But there has been so much talk of the Spirit, especially at the time of Hegelian idealism—absolute Spirit, universal Spirit, Spirit for itself, outside of itself, in itself. . . . But today we realize from the consequences that the Spirit was never so far away and forgotten in the Christian West as in that period.

2. *The Office of Preaching*

In light of what we have said, I believe that two fundamental teachings can be drawn from the reading of the story of Pentecost given by Luke. The first teaching is that the primary activity of the Church is the proclamation of the dead and risen Christ: "This man . . . you killed. . . . But God raised him up, releasing him from the throes of death . . . ." (Acts 2:23-24). When a baby comes into the light, a shriek or a wail indicates that it is alive and breathing. In the same way the Church makes its entrance into the world on the day of Pentecost, emitting a cry that makes it recognizable as a living Church. This cry is the *kerygma* pronounced by Peter in the name of all the apostles: "Therefore let the whole house of Israel know for certain that God has made him both Lord and Messiah, this Jesus whom you crucified" (Acts 2:36). It is as if Peter had said: "Let the whole world know for certain . . . ." There is an extraordinary force and authority in his words that surely does not come from someone who shortly before had been afraid to face a simple maidservant.

This fact—that the Church exists first of all for proclaiming the word—is quite clear to everyone and has been inculcated in all the most important recent documents of the Magisterium: in the decree on missionary activity *(Ad gentes)* of Vatican II, in Paul VI's encyclical *Evangelii nuntiandi,* in the apostolic exhortation to the laity *Christifideles laici.* There is nothing to add to this incredibly rich mass of texts. I would only like to put forth a few reflections that arise from the fact that I find myself directly employed in the proclamation of the word and have seen, so to speak, how things are out in the field.

Where do the most alive and most valid energies of the Church go? What does the office of preaching represent among all the possible activities and destinations of young priests? I seem to notice one serious drawback—that only the elements that remain after the choice for academic studies, administration, diplomacy, and youth formation are dedicated to preaching. What does the office of preaching represent in the life of pastors? St. Gregory the Great wrote:

> There are people who would listen to the good word but preachers are lacking. The world is full of priests, and still those who work in the vineyard of the Lord are hard to find. We have assumed the priestly office but we do not perform the works that the office brings along with it. . . . We have immersed ourselves in earthly affairs and it is one thing that we have assumed with the priestly office and quite another thing that we show with our deeds. We abandon the ministry of preaching and we are called bishops, but perhaps rather to our condemnation, given that we possess the honorific title and not the qualities.[5]

Perhaps St. Gregory alludes to some abuse particular to his own time that no longer exists today. I hope so, but even so his words do not cease to make us reflect.

Another reflection that I would like to put forth has to do with the relation between preaching, or the proclamation of the Word, and theological activity in the Church. I was struck reading the affirmations of two noted contemporary theologians. Henri de Lubac has written: "The *ministerium praedicationis* is not the vulgarization of a doctrinal teaching in a more abstract form that would be prior and superior to it. It is, on the contrary, the doctrinal teaching itself in its highest form. This was true of the first Christian preaching, that of the apostles, and it is equally true of the preaching of their successors in the Church: the Fathers, the Doctors, and our Pastors in the present time."[6] Hans Urs von Balthasar, in his turn, speaks of the "mission of preaching in the Church, to which the theological mission itself is subordinate."[7] These affirmations struck me because it seems that the relation that exists in fact between these two activities, at least in the opinion of the majority of the people and of the priests themselves, is precisely the opposite—that preaching would only be the vulgarization of a more technical and abstract teaching prior and superior to it, namely, theology.

St. Paul, the model of all preachers, the "preacher of the truth" par excellence, certainly puts preaching before everything and subordinates everything to it. By preaching he did theology and not a theology from which the more elementary things could be pulled out to be transmitted to the simple faithful in preaching. "For Christ did not send me to baptize but to preach the gospel . . . ." (1 Cor 1:17); he maintained that to preach the Gospel is more important and necessary even than baptism. "Woe to me," he also said, "if I do not preach it" (1 Cor 9:16).

In fact, what is at stake here is the very conversion of men and their coming to faith. Faith depends on proclamation: *fides ex auditu* (Rom 10:17). The word is the "place" of the decisive encounter between God and man. The liturgy is an essential element in the life of the Church but it comes after. A beautiful liturgy can edify, can help anyone who already has faith to grow, but it is unusual that a non-believer (supposing that he participates) feels "cut to the heart" as happens instead to those who listened to Peter speak on Pentecost (cf. Acts 2:37).

What is the reason for the alarming defection of Catholics to other established churches or even to "fundamentalist" Christian sects? Is it really because these people know what fundamentalism is or love fundamentalism in some special way? If not, by what then are they attracted? They are simply drawn by a "fundamental" word that more than anything puts them in contact with the person of Jesus. To be sure, it is an error to abandon the "catholic" Church, where there is the fullness of faith and means of salvation, for other churches or groups that bring them to the first or even the second conversion but that cannot always bring them to the perfection of the Christian life and to what we normally call sanctity.

But the problem of the sects and defections from the Catholic Church is not solved by issuing warnings or, worse, by suspending all ecumenical dialogue with them. Nor can such defection be prevented by instructing these people once they already live, for the most part, far from the Church without any real contact with it. We must put forth in the Catholic Church, in a catholic way, enriched by all the immense reserves of experience and doctrine of the tradition, a proclamation with the same force and essentiality as the one they find elsewhere, but with the additional guarantee of authenticity and completeness that only the great tradition of the Church can give. A proclamation that, like that of Jesus, does not begin with duties and commandments but with the gift of God, with grace, not from what man must do but from what God has done for him. Peter did not begin to speak, saying immediately "Repent and be baptized!" No, first he proclaimed Christ crucified and risen and made Lord; then, when hearts were open and ready to receive it, he launched the appeal to penitence and change of life.

A change of mentality with respect to the message, a new courage, a pentecostal spirit, is necessary. One encouraging sign of this change of mind is the call addressed to the laity, in a recent document of the Magisterium, that is inspired by the saying of Christ: "You too go into my vineyard . . . ." (Matt 20:4). One chapter of this letter is entitled, "The hour has come for a re-evangelization." In it one reads, "The Church today ought to take *a giant step forward* in her evangelization effort, and enter into *a new stage of history* in her missionary dynamism. In a world where the lessening of distance makes the world increasingly smaller, the church community ought to strengthen the bonds among its members, exchange vital energies and means, and commit itself as a group to a unique and common mission of proclaiming and living the Gospel."[8] It is through this mission that "even in our times there is no lack of a fruitful manifestation of various charisms among the faithful, women and men."[9] We have here an echo of the speech of Peter on the day of Pentecost, when he applies to the Church the prophecy of Joel:

> "I will pour out a portion of my spirit upon all flesh.
> Your sons and your daughters shall prophesy. . . .
> Indeed, upon my servants and my handmaids
>   I will pour out a portion of my spirit in those days,
>   and they shall prophesy" (Acts 2:17-18).

3. *To Preach the Gospel in the Holy Spirit*

The second teaching that comes from the Lukan account of Pentecost has already emerged from what has been said. It is not enough to renew the contents, the forms, and the style of the evangelization or to involve the laity in it too. The decisive factor is whether the proclamation is made "in the power of the Holy Spirit" or without it. "My message and my proclamation," Paul writes, "were not with persuasive [words of] wisdom, but with a demonstration of spirit and power, so that your faith might rest not on human wisdom but on the power of God" (1 Cor 2:4-5).

The First Letter of Peter defines the apostles as "those who preached the good news to you [through] the holy Spirit . . . ." (1:12). The Gospel is the *content* of the proclamation, the Holy Spirit is its *method,* the way or the mode, the operative principle. Paul VI defines it as "the principal agent" of evangelization.[10]

Speaking prophetically, or "in the Spirit," takes place wherever the saying of Jesus "For it will not be you who speak but the Spirit of your Father speaking through you" (Matt 10:20) is realized. Luke, in the parallel passage, specifies that this "Spirit of the Father" will be a "a wisdom in speaking that all your adversaries will be powerless to resist or refute" (Luke 21:15). The adversaries in this case will be able to kill the witness of Christ, but not to confute him, as the example of Stephen shows. Why were the words of Peter on the day of Pentecost so effective unless the Spirit of God was speaking in them? What pierced the hearts of those three thousand persons and "convinced them they had sinned" if not the Spirit of God?

Therefore, as we set out to proclaim the word of God, we must make sure that the Spirit is with us and, above all, that we are with the Spirit. How? The first means that the Acts of the Apostles suggests to us is *prayer.* The Holy Spirit came upon the apostles while they "devoted themselves with one accord to prayer" (Acts 1:14) and Jesus says that the heavenly Father will "give the Holy Spirit to those who ask him" (Luke 11:13).

Another important means is *obedience,* especially in the sense of submission and adherence to the will of God. God gives the Holy Spirit "to those who obey him" (Acts 5:32). God gives his power and authority to those who accept his will through to the end. The Holy Spirit cannot act in someone who is still attached to his own will. Only one who heeds God—that is, obeys him—is heeded by men.

The third and last means is *love* for those to whom one has been sent to proclaim the Gospel. God speaks through love. The "breath" of God is a whisper of love. Why does God speak to men? Because He has given to them His Son Jesus Christ? It is written, "For God so loved the world that he gave his only Son . . . ." (John 3:16). The one proclaiming the good news must enter into this law and this "economy" of love. He must love human beings, the aloof, the sinners, in order to be able to give to them the word of life. Jesus can only give himself through love, not through reproofs and judgments almost hurled at the people. To do so would be to distort the very meaning of the Gospel. What a contrast there is between God's attitude towards the inhabitants of Nineveh and Jonah's! "You are concerned over the plant," God says to Jonah, "which cost you no labor and which you did not raise. . . . And should not I be concerned over Nineveh, the great city, in which there are more than a hundred and twenty thousand persons who cannot distinguish their right hand from their left . . . ?" (Jonah 4:10-11). Although Jonah had gone to preach to the Ninevites, he did not love them, and God had to go through more trouble to convert him, the preacher, than to convert the inhabitants of Nineveh. Before speaking out the word of God or expounding to others his will, it is very useful and healthy to collect yourself and ask: But do I love these people as God loves them?

Love is the "warm breath," the spiritual fire, that transports the word, and we know that love is given "through the Holy Spirit" (Rom 5:5). Also and especially in this sense—that is, to the extent that it is love—the Holy Spirit is the power of the word, the secret of proclaiming it.

Our situation today with respect to this proclamation has several things in common with the situation in which the apostles found themselves after the threats of the Sanhedrin. As soon as they were set free, Peter and John went to their comrades and reported what the high priests and elders had said—namely, that they must no longer speak to anyone in the name of Jesus. What did the apostles do in these circumstances? The first thing they did was to pray with the community. They said, "Enable your servants to speak your word with all boldness, as you stretch forth [your] hand to heal, and signs and wonders are done through the name of your holy servant Jesus" (Acts 4:29-30). Then the Holy Spirit came again as on Pentecost and once again "they were all filled with the holy Spirit and continued to speak the word of God with boldness" (Acts 4:31). As on the day of Pentecost, the Holy Spirit was given to enable the Church to proclaim the Word with *courage*.

Since, as I was saying, our contemporary situation has much in common with that of the apostles, let us too unite ourselves to their prayer, let us pray like them: Come, Holy Spirit! Truly, today also "in this city," in this our world, "Herod and Pontius Pilate with the Gentiles and the people of Israel" are allied together against your holy servant Jesus. Today also all the powers—culture, prosperity, ideology, what is outside of man and what is within him—conspire practically to eliminate from the midst of human beings God, Jesus Christ and his Church. Lord, turn your gaze upon us, today also extend your hand so that cures, miracles, and wonders are performed in the name of Jesus, because we have become distracted, deaf, and hard of heart and the words no longer suffice. Let us have the courage to ask you again for signs and prodigies not for us, but for your glory and for the spread of your kingdom. It is true, you have told us that such signs are useful "for unbelievers" (1 Cor 14:22). But our world is again—or has become once more—in great part unbelieving. For this reason we need some of your signs that might convince the world or at least reclaim its attention. You have promised us to work together with those who preach and to confirm their words "through accompanying signs" (Mark 16:20).

Today also, as at the beginning, your word falls upon a world in which a babble of voices—of even the most absurd religious propositions—chase and collide with one another. How will your word make itself heard above the human shouting? Today also renew for us your consoling promise: "But you will receive power when the holy Spirit comes upon you, and you will be my witnesses . . . ." (Acts 1:8).

NOTES

1. See Friedrich Baumgaertel's contribution to the article on *pneuma, pneumatikos* in the *Theological Dictionary of the New Testament,* vol. 6, ed. Gerhard Friedrich, trans. Geoffrey Bromiley (Grand Rapids, Mich.: Eerdmans, 1968) 359–68.
2. See *Stoicorum veterum fragmenta,* ed. Hans von Arnim (Dubuque: W.C. Brown Reprint Library, 1964) I, 137; II, 1035.
3. Ibid., II, 310, 416.
4. St. Gregory Nazianzen, "On the Holy Spirit," *The Nicene and Post-Nicene Fathers,* Second Series, vol. 7, trans. Charles Gordon Browne and James Edward Swallow (Grand Rapids, Mich.: Eerdmans, 1983) 326–7. [31.28]

5. Gregory the Great, *Omelie sui Vangeli,* XVII, 3 (PL 76, 1139s).

6. Henri de Lubac, *Exegese medievale,* vol. I, part 2 (Paris, 1959) 670. The first of four volumes of this work has been published as *Medieval Exegesis, Volume 1: The Four Senses of Scripture,* trans. Mark Sebanc (Grand Rapids, Mich.: Eerdmans, 1998). The second volume will contain the passage cited here and in the next note.

7. Hans Urs von Balthasar, *Contemplative Prayer,* cited in Lubac.

8. *Christfideles Laici,* in *The Post-Synodal Apostolic Exhortations of John Paul II,* ed. J. Michael Miller, C.S.B. (Huntington, Ind.: Our Sunday Visitor Publishing Division, 1998) 412. [35.5]

9. Ibid., 394. [24.3]

10. Pope Paul VI, *On Evangelization in the Modern World (Evangelii nuntiandi)* (Washington, D.C.: United States Catholic Conference, 1976) 57. [75]

Chapter III

"He Breathed on Them and Said, 'Receive the Holy Spirit'"

The Johannine Pentecost and the Spirit of Truth

The New Testament does not contain the account of only one Pentecost but of two. There is a Lukan Pentecost, the one described in the Acts of the Apostles, and there is a Johannine Pentecost, described in John 20:22, when Jesus breathed on his disciples and said, "Receive the holy Spirit." This Johannine Pentecost takes place in the same location as Luke's account, in the Cenaculum, the Upper Room, but not at the same time. In fact, it happens on the very evening of Easter and not fifty days after it.

This fact of a double narrative of the coming of the Holy Spirit was already noticed by the Fathers of the Church. "Look here, my brothers and sisters," said St. Augustine, "someone may ask me: 'Why did he give the Holy Spirit twice?' What he gave was one, he himself who gave it was one, he gave it to the unity, and yet he gave it twice. The first time, when he said to his disciples after he had risen again, 'Receive the Holy Spirit.' And he breathed into their faces. There you have it once. Next he promises that he is still going to send the Holy Spirit, and he says 'You will receive the power of the Holy Spirit coming down upon you' (Acts 1:8); and in another place, 'Stay in the city for I am to fulfill the promise of my Father, which you have heard, he said, from my mouth.' After he had ascended, and they had spent ten days there, he sent the Holy Spirit. That's the solemnity of Pentecost that is coming."[1]

The Fathers usually explained this "anomaly" by saying that the gift of the Spirit spoken of in John was a partial gift, restricted either in content or the number of those receiving it, a kind of first fruit with respect to the more complete and universal gift lavished fifty days later.[2]

Today a simpler explanation is given for this fact. The two accounts of the coming of the Holy Spirit correspond to two different modes of conceiving and representing the gift of the Spirit, two modes that do not exclude one another, indeed that complement one another, but that need not be forced to harmonize. Luke and John describe—from two different angles and with two different theological preoccupations—the same fundamental event of the history of salvation: the outpouring of the Spirit made possible by the paschal sacrifice of Christ. This outpouring manifested itself at different moments and in different ways. Luke, who sees the Holy Spirit as a gift made to the Church for its mission, stresses one of these moments, the one that took place fifty days after Easter on the day when the Jews were celebrating the conclusion of the feast of Pentecost. John, who sees the Spirit as the principle of the new life welling up from the paschal sacrifice of Christ, stresses the earliest manifestations of it which happened on the very day of Easter. In time and in space, Easter and Pentecost draw near to one another.

There is, therefore, a way of describing the coming of the Holy Spirit that is proper to and characteristic of John. Right from the beginning of the Fourth Gospel, a promise is made: there will be a baptism of the Holy Spirit (cf. John 1:33). This promise is confirmed and made specific in the discussion with the Samaritan woman about living water (cf. John 4:14). Later it is placed in close relation with the "glorification" of Jesus (cf. John 7:39), which means, as we know, his glorious death and not only his ascension into heaven. It is unthinkable that John might end his Gospel without having shown to his readers the fulfillment of this promise, or that he might refer them for such a fulfillment to another book of the New Testament, such as Acts, which he probably did not even know. The entire Gospel of John, therefore, requires a Pentecost as its conclusion.

We have some confirmation of this from the history and liturgy of the Church. We know that in the first centuries of the Church there were two fundamental modes of understanding the feast of Pentecost, just as there were two fundamental modes of understanding and celebrating Easter. According to one of these—affirmed later and become universal right down to our day—Pentecost was the feast of the descent of the Holy Spirit which took place on the *fiftieth day* after Easter. According to the other way, which is older, Pentecost was the feast of the *fifty days* following Easter and it commemorated the spiritual presence, or the presence "according to the Spirit," of Jesus among his disciples after the resurrection. This presence was seen as the first fruit of the new life and a foreshadowing of eternal life. For Tertullian, for example, Pentecost is that time

> wherein, too, the resurrection of Jesus was repeatedly proved among the disciples, and the hope of the advent of the Lord indirectly pointed to, in that, at that time, when He had been received back into the heavens, the angels told the apostles that "He would so come, as He had withal ascended into the heavens."[3]

According to this conception—linked to the Johannine tradition like the Quartodeciman practice of celebrating Easter on the date of Passover—the gift of the Holy Spirit *inaugurated* Pentecost, whereas according to the other conception, based on the Lukan account of Acts, it *concluded* it.

1. *The Holy Spirit in John and in the Synoptics: Novelty and Continuity*

Now let us see what the Johannine Pentecost adds to our knowledge of the Holy Spirit and of its role in the story of salvation. The best method to assemble the rich and varied revelation of the New Testament on the Holy Spirit is what we might define as "superimposition." This is the method used, for example, to illustrate visually the physiology of the human body. Sometimes one sees graphics composed of different transparent sheets, bound together and placed on top of each other. On each sheet, one part or organ of the human body is drawn with a different color: the skeletal system on one, on another the nervous system, on a third the circulatory system, and so on. Looking at these graphics separately, one sees clearly how that particular organ or system is made and how it is distributed throughout the body. Then, placing one above the other, one sees the human body delineate itself with ever greater complexity until, once all the sheets have been superimposed, one sees the entire body with all the organs that compose it.

To apply this method of superimposition to the study of the New Testament doctrine of the Holy Spirit means first to analyze in isolation the pneumatology of each individual author or book of the New Testament—of the Synoptics, John, and Paul—in order next, in a second step, to put together the results and to have thereby a complete vision of the whole revelation on the Holy Spirit. Such a method is opposed *both* to passing indiscriminately from one author to another, from one "system" to another, collecting a little evidence and a few words from this one and a little evidence and a few words from that one, with the risk of obtaining a hybrid and artificial image of New Testament pneumatology *and* to stopping short of a single system and limiting oneself to pointing out only the differences between one author and the other without ever attempting a synthesis. At the time of the Fathers, the first tendency, the "synthetic," prevailed; today the second, "analytic," prevails instead. Today, one insists more on the diversity of the human authors; rather than on the identity of the divine author of Scripture.

In these meditations, by applying the method I have called superimposition, I would like to shed as much light as possible on the Holy Spirit by examining separately and then putting together the essentials of what Luke, John, and Paul have understood about the Spirit since they are the three richest authors in this respect. Thus we will not in the end have many different revelations but a single revelation that grows and is enriched in time, proceeding from one self-same Spirit like the different colors of the spectrum that, when combined, form the great light of the Holy Spirit. In this chapter let us try to pick out the fundamental message concerning the Holy Spirit that John transmits to us in the Fourth Gospel. Let us superimpose John on Luke to see what new lineaments of the person of the Holy Spirit emerge.

In Luke's understanding the Holy Spirit appears to us as the divine power, operating first in Jesus and later in the Church, that enables the mission to be brought to completion, overcoming every obstacle. The great novelty to be noted in John, with respect to Luke and the other two Synoptics, is that the Holy Spirit not only enables the fulfillment of supplementary actions, not only serves to *carry* salvation to the ends of the earth. It *constitutes* salvation! It is the principle of the new existence at work in the world since the coming and paschal sacrifice of Christ. It is not, therefore, something supplementary and accidental but something essential. It is the new life, the life in Christ. The "Spirit of life" is also the life of the spirit!

This results clearly from the fact that John does not speak much of the Spirit who causes marvelous actions to be performed and distributes charisms. He does not even insist on saying that Jesus receives the Spirit or that he works in the Spirit because, Jesus is, rather, for him the one who gives the Spirit and who "will baptize with the holy Spirit" (cf. John 1:33). For John the Spirit is an interior principle that acts "in" whoever receives it and not only "through" him. This is a huge step forward with respect to the Old Testament to which the Synoptics had remained substantially tied. Here we touch with our hand the novelty brought by the coming of Christ, even in the revelation of the Holy Spirit.

Nevertheless, it is not quite right to say that there are no points of contact between John's vision of the Spirit and Luke's. John deepens the vision of the Synoptics, but he does not deny it. A clear point of contact exists between the two in John 20:22, which we have called the Johannine Pentecost. The Holy Spirit that Jesus here gives to the apostles is clearly for the sake of their mission: "As the Father has sent me, so I send you." After saying this, he breathed on them and said, "Receive the Holy Spirit." The gesture of breathing or blowing recalls Gen 2:7 and Ezek 37:9 and thus represents the Spirit as giver of life and principle of the new creation, but the words that accompany the gesture represent the same Spirit as the force that will enable the apostles to carry out their mission and will confer upon them the power to take away sins. They represent it, in other words, as a prophetic and ministerial Spirit.

The difference between Luke and John, if anything, is that in John the Spirit that enables the mission is the same Spirit who gives life. The prophetic force and the authority to take away sins are one aspect of the Spirit who is the principle of new life, and they derive from it. There is not a prophetic and charismatic Spirit that does some things and performs some functions and another Spirit of truth and life that does other things. This will be even clearer in Paul, for whom the same Holy Spirit who distributes charisms is the one who pours love and the gifts of charity into hearts (cf. Rom 5:5, 1 Cor 12–13).

In the Creed the Church itself has made the most beautiful synthesis of the biblical doctrine of the two dimensions—prophetic and vivifying—of the action of the Holy Spirit. When it wished to define, along with the divinity of the Holy Spirit, its principal prerogatives, what did the Council of Constantinople of 381 do? To the article already present in the Nicene Creed—"And I believe in the Holy Spirit"—it added the phrase—"the Lord, the giver of Life . . . He has spoken through the prophets." In this way, perhaps without directly formulating it, simply by adhering to the Bible, the Fathers miraculously captured the double function of the Spirit to be a "vivifying" Spirit and one that has spoken through the prophets and speaks today through the Church. In such a way, the two lines along which the revelation on the Holy Spirit were developing converged in the heart of the Church's faith. The great torch of the Holy Spirit was finally inserted into the candelabra of the Church, the symbol of faith.[4]

2. The Holy Spirit, Principle of the Birth and Growth of the Church

Having stated precisely this point that allows us to see a continuity and not a break between the Synoptics and John, let us now consider better the new aspects that have emerged in John's pneumatology. We can divide the passages in John that speak of the Spirit as the constitutive principle of salvation into two series. The first series illuminates the Holy Spirit's role in *becoming*—that is, in the very establishment and birth of the Church—whereas the second series (John 14–16) illuminates the role of the Holy Spirit in its *being*—that is, in the enduring or functioning of the Church, in other words, in its growth and life.

To the first series belong all those texts that speak of the *Holy Spirit as active principle of the new birth,* variously described as born "of spirit" (John 3:6), "of God" (John 1:13), or "from above" (John 3:3). In these passages the Spirit is both the subject or the agent that calls forth the new spiritual birth and also its object, that in which the new birth and the new life consist. This new existence "of the Spirit" springs from the fact that the Spirit puts the one who believes and is baptized in vital contact with the

Redeemer and through him with the world of God, with the "above." He makes him enter into another sphere by giving him the "knowledge" of God and Christ and with that "eternal life." John 19:30 and 34—which speak of the Spirit that Jesus "handed over" dying on the cross and of the blood and water that are the signs and sacramental symbols of it—also refer in a symbolic way to this initial moment of the life of the believer and of the Church (cf. 1 John 5:5-8).

To the second series of passages, which speak of the *Spirit as cause of growth,* belong the sayings concerning the Paraclete in chapters 14–16 of the Fourth Gospel and even the two passages on spiritual anointing (cf. 1 John 2:20-27). It is useful to read these texts, which are bracketed by other discourses, straight through and as a whole, according to John's style of developing a theme by returning again and again to it. Only in this way can one fully appreciate the great Johannine revelation concerning the Holy Spirit. Let us listen to it again, therefore, as if it were one uninterrupted discourse, italicizing the recurrent titles of the Spirit and signifying with a new paragraph the gap between one verse and another.

"And I will ask the Father, and he will give you another *Advocate* to be with you always, the *Spirit of truth,* which the world cannot accept, because it neither sees nor knows it. But you know it because it remains with you, and will be in you. . . .

"The *Advocate,* the *holy Spirit* that the Father will send in my name—he will teach you everything and remind you of all that [I] told you. . . .

"When the *Advocate* comes whom I will send you from the Father, the *Spirit of Truth* that proceeds from the Father, he will testify to me. . . .

"But I tell you the truth, it is better for you that I go. For if I do not go, the *Advocate* will not come to you. But if I go, I will send him to you. And when he comes he will convict the world in regard to sin and righteousness and condemnation: sin, because they do not believe in me; righteousness, because I am going to the Father and you will no longer see me; condemnation, because the ruler of this world has been condemned.

"I have much more to tell you, but you cannot bear it now. But when he comes, the *Spirit of Truth,* he will guide you to all truth. He will not speak on his own, but he will speak what he hears, and will declare to you the things that are coming. He will glorify me because he will take from what is mine and declare it to you. Everything that the Father has is mine; for this reason I told you that he will take from what is mine and declare it to you" (John 14:16-17, 26; 15:26, 16:7-15).

In all these passages the background problem is no longer how to be "born" into the new life but how the believer, once he has come there, might "remain" and grow in this life, how the Church can face the opposition of the world and come out of it victorious, and how the Church can continue to remain in contact with Jesus Christ and even grow in its knowledge. The background, therefore, is the life of the Church in history.

To such texts of the Fourth Gospel are connected those of the First Letter of John. The anointing that "teaches you about everything" (John 2:27), in fact, recalls what is said in John 14:26 of the Spirit who "will teach you everything," just as the phrase "the Spirit is truth" recalls the epithet "Spirit of truth" that recurs in the Gospel.

3. The Spirit of Truth

Now let us set out, as usual, to discover the relevance for our time of this Johannine revelation concerning the Spirit, trying to see in its light the situation and needs of the Church today. In order to remain as faithful as possible to the evangelist's intention, let us concentrate our attention on the two titles for the Holy Spirit dearest to John: Spirit of truth and Paraclete or Advocate.

In order to realize what the expression "Spirit of truth" means, it is necessary to know what "truth" *(aletheia)* signifies in the Fourth Gospel. "Like *aletheia*, it *[Pneuma]* denotes the reality of God." For this reason, to worship God "in Spirit and truth" (John 4:24) means "to worship in the sphere of God and no longer in that of the *kosmos,* in reality and no longer in the realm of mere appearance."[5] Therefore, to worship God in Spirit and truth means not to worship him in human fashion bound to human places and modes but to worship him in his own sphere, made accessible in Christ and, after him, in the Spirit. To worship God by means of God just as, moreover, we love God by means of God!

The sense of the word "truth" alternates in John between the divine *reality* and the *knowledge* of the divine reality, between an ontological or objective meaning and a gnosiological or subjective one. The traditional interpretation, especially the Catholic one, has understood "truth" above all in the second sense, *of knowledge and formulation of the truth,* in other words, in the dogmatic sense. The Spirit guides the Church to a full knowledge of the implications of revelation through councils, the Magisterium, the tradition.

This is an aspect of the action of the Spirit of truth—the most important, if you like—but not the only one. There is a more personal and existential aspect that we must equally bear in mind and it is this: the Holy Spirit leads us to an ever more intimate and profound contact with the *reality* of God, gives us access to the very life of Christ. It is the active principle of our experience, not only of our knowledge, of the reality of God. St. Irenaeus calls the Holy Spirit our "communion with God,"[6] and St. Basil says that "through the Spirit we become intimate with God."[7] In the Holy Spirit we enter into direct contact with God without created intermediaries. We no longer know God "through hearsay" or through go-betweens but "in person." Not from outside but from inside.

The action of the Spirit of truth, therefore, is not limited only to a few rare and solemn moments of the life of the Church. There exists an institutional action, exercised through the institutions (councils, bishops, popes) of the Church, and there exists an inner action, daily and uninterrupted, in the heart of every believer. "It remains with you, and will be in you" (John 14:17). This is that anointing "that comes from the holy one," that gives wisdom, that remains in us, that teaches everything and makes us stand firm in the truth (1 John 20, 27). In this sense too, the Holy Spirit appears the "mighty Teacher" of the Church.[8]

This teaching that the Spirit imparts in the innermost recesses of every believer must be placed under the discernment and judgment of the community and especially its pastor, as John himself says (cf. 1 John 4:1-6) so that the "Spirit of truth" is distinguished from the "spirit of error." But the fact that this interior and personal guide of the Spirit can be subject to deception and abuse does not justify suppressing it or regarding it with suspicion. If the saints became what they were, it was above all through submission to this secret guide that moment by moment suggested to them what was most pleasing to God and conformed best to the Spirit of Christ.

All that helps us to see with different eyes the tradition of the Church, too. Why is the tradition of the Church called "living" if not because in it the Holy Spirit lives and works? Why is it likened to a vessel not only containing the precious liquor of revelation but even "renewing its youth,"[9] unless, once again, because in it the Holy Spirit is at work? The Holy Spirit is the soul of the tradition. If it is removed or forgotten, what remains of the tradition is only the dead "letter." If the very life of Jesus and the Eucharist itself are "of no avail" (John 6:63) without the Spirit that gives life, what must be said of the tradition?

This allows us to understand the true cause of the painful crisis experienced by the Catholic Church in the wake of Vatican II and that led to the schism of Lefebvre. The tradition that was defended—and in the name of which some separated from the Church—was a tradition no longer with the Holy Spirit, no longer with any actual and vital relation to it. A tradition reduced, in fact, to "flesh that is good for nothing" and to the "letter [that] brings death" (2 Cor 3:6). The true problem and the true weak point, often passed unobserved in all this affair, was the complete forgetting of the Holy Spirit. The experience demonstrates that you can cultivate a great devotion to the Holy Spirit, even ask every day for his "seven gifts," and nevertheless, eviscerate their significance, holding the Holy Spirit carefully outside of the true and actual life of the Church, demanding the he adapt to our truth, instead of we to his.

4. *The "Advocate"*

The other recurrent title of the Spirit in John is that of Paraclete. This name has different shades of meaning: defender, advocate, counselor. . . . But all of them indicate an action on behalf of those who believe. In him Jesus himself continues to be alongside his Church. "Another" Advocate, Jesus calls him. During his life on earth he was himself the Advocate: "Come to me, all you who labor and are burdened, and I will give you rest,"[10] he said (Matt 11:28). When he promises the Advocate, it is almost as if he had said: "Go to him all who labor and are burdened and he will give you rest!"

At this moment, however, the most important thing is not so much to explain the meaning of the title Advocate, as much as to receive the invitation of Christ and to experience the consolation of the Holy Spirit. The background against which the action of the Paraclete is presented to us is the clash with the world. The world, however, is not only outside us; it also works inside us in wicked tendencies, resistance, weaknesses, sin. Such a mass of negativity and evil that at times it seems impossible to resist it.

The Holy Spirit plays in us a role exactly the opposite of the one played by the spirit of evil. The same John, who calls the Holy Spirit the Defender, calls Satan "the accuser" (Rev 12:10). The Holy Spirit defends the faithful and "intercedes" ceaselessly for them before God with "inexpressible groanings" (Rom 8:26ff.); the spirit of evil accuses believers "before God day and night." He accuses the faithful before God and accuses God before the faithful. But how much the defender is infinitely stronger and victorious than the accuser! With him we can conquer every temptation and transform the temptation itself into victory.

How does this "perfect consoler" *(consolator optime),* as a liturgical hymn defines him, console us? Is it in the same way as human beings usually console, with words? No, he is in himself the consolation, he effects what he signifies, because he is spirit not flesh, God, not man (cf. Isa 31:3). He consoles by making the words that Jesus spoke to his disciples when he was with them resound in our hearts: "In the world you will have trouble, but take courage, I have conquered the world" (John 16:33). He consoles by testifying in our spirits that we are children of God (cf. Rom 8:16). The apostle Paul experienced this divine consolation in tribulations, so much so that he called God "the father of compassion and God of all encouragement"[11] (cf. 2 Cor 1:3ff.). In the beginning the whole Church had this experience of the Spirit who consoles. It is written, "It was being built up and walked in the fear of the Lord, and with the consolation of the holy Spirit it grew in great numbers" (Acts 9:31).

44

5. *Thirst for the Holy Spirit or Fear of the Holy Spirit?*

"On the last and greatest day of the feast, Jesus stood up and exclaimed, 'Let anyone who thirsts come to me and drink'" (John 7:37). And the evangelist John comments, "He said this in reference to the Spirit . . . ." (John 7:39). The first condition for receiving the Holy Spirit is not the merits and virtues but desire, vital need, thirst. The words of Jesus echo those of Isaiah, who said,

> All you who are thirsty,
> come to the water!
> You who have no money,
> come, receive grain and eat (55:1).

The practical problem about the Holy Spirit lies right here. Are we thirsty for the Holy Spirit or do we have instead an unacknowledged fear of him? We intuit that if the Holy Spirit comes, he cannot leave everything in our existence as he finds it. He could even make us do "strange" things that we are not ready to accept. He has never left those upon whom he has come sedentary and inactive. Whoever the Holy Spirit touches, the Holy spirit changes! Thus, our prayer for having the Spirit sometimes resembles the prayer Augustine addressed to God before his conversion: "Grant me chastity and self-control, but please not yet."[12] We are tempted to say, "Come, Holy Spirit, come . . . , but not right now and especially no strangeness and singularity! Isn't God order, decorum, composure and equilibrium?"

If the apostles could have chosen and decided for themselves the way the Spirit, after a little while, should have manifested himself, they would never, ever have chosen to begin to speak in unknown tongues, exposing themselves to the ridicule of the people who said "They have had too much new wine" (Acts 2:13). And yet it was in this way that what happened, happened. Therefore, in the first place let us ask the Holy Spirit to take away our fear of him. Let us say, "Come, come, Holy Spirit! Come now, come as you wish. Bend, warm, cure, water, burn, renew."

On Easter evening Jesus breathed upon his disciples and said: "Receive the Holy Spirit," almost begging them to accept his gift. In this gesture the great prophecy of Ezekiel concerning the dry bones is fulfilled: "Then he said to me: Prophesy to the spirit, prophesy, son of man, and say to the spirit: Thus says the LORD God: From the four winds come, O spirit, and breathe into these slain that they may come to life" (Ezek 37:9). The son of man is now no longer Ezekiel, a prophet, but the Son of Man par excellence, the very one who is also the Son of God. He is the one who cries to the Spirit, who calls him and breathes him out. He does not call him from outside of himself, "from the four winds," but from himself, from his open side. He has not done this only once, on Easter evening, but does it continually. Even today he stands before the disciples and the Church and repeats his pressing invitation: "Receive the Holy Spirit!" Let us expose our faces and our souls to this breath of life and let it quicken and renew us. Even today, if the entire Church received this powerful breath, if the Spirit entered in force in all its realities, it "would rise and walk" and would newly be "a great army without end."

NOTES

1. St. Augustine, *Sermons, The Works of St. Augustine,* Part III, vol. 7, trans. Edmund Hill, O.P. (New Rochelle, N.Y.: New City Press, 1993) 241. [265.9,8] See also St. Augustine, *Tractates on the Gospel of John 55–111,* vol. 4, *The Fathers of the Church,* vol. 90, trans. John W. Rettig (Washington, D.C.: The Catholic University Press, 1994) 88–92. [74.2]
2. See *The Works of St. Cyril of Jerusalem,* vol. 2, in *The Fathers of the Church,* vol. 64, trans. Leo McCauley, S.J. (Washington, D.C.: The Catholic University Press, 1970) 104–5. [Catechesis 17.12–14]. See also Cyril the Alexandrian, *Commentary on John* 12.1 (PG 74, 709–22).
3. Tertullian, "On Baptism," *The Anti-Nicene Fathers,* vol. 3, ed. Roberts and Donaldson (New York: Scribner's, 1925) 678. [19.2]
4. St. Gregory Nazianzen, "On the Holy Spirit," *The Nicene and Post-Nicene Fathers,* Second Series, vol. 7, trans. Charles Gordon Browne and James Edward Swallow (Grand Rapids, Mich.: Eerdmans, 1983) 247. [12.6]
5. Eduard Schweizer, in the *Theological Dictionary of the New Testament,* vol. 6, ed. Gerhard Friedrich, trans. Geoffrey Bromiley (Grand Rapids, Mich.: Eerdmans, 1968) 439.

6. St. Irenaeus, "Against Heresies," *The Anti-Nicene Fathers*, vol. 1, ed. Rev. Alexander Roberts and James Donaldson (New York: Scribner's, 1908) 527. [5.1.1]

7. St. Basil the Great, *On the Holy Spirit*, trans. David Anderson (Crestwood, N.Y.: St. Vladimir's Seminary Press, 1980) 77. [19.49]

8. St. Cyril of Jerusalem, *Catecheses*, 88. [16.19]

9. St. Irenaeus, 458. [3.24.1]

10. In Italian the word translated as "Advocate" in the NAB is sometimes translated as "Consolatore," Consoler, and the phrase "I will give you rest" is "vi consolero," I will console you. The pun is lost in English.

11. Where the NAB has "encouragement," the Italian Bible has "consolazione," consolation.

12. St. Augustine, *Confessions*, trans. Maria Boulding. O.S.B., *The Works of St. Augustine*, Part I, vol. 1, ed. John Rotelle, O.S.A. (Hyde Park, N.Y.: New City Press, 1997) 198. [8.7]

Chapter IV

"But One and the Same Spirit Produces All of These"

The Pauline Pentecost and the "Person" of the Holy Spirit

In reading St. Paul, in what sense can we speak not only of a pneumatology but also of a Pentecost—that is, not only of a *doctrine* of the Spirit but also of an *event* of the Spirit? In the Letter to the Ephesians, we read:

> But grace was given to each of us according to the measure of Christ's gift. Therefore, it says:
> "He ascended on high and took prisoners captive;
>   He gave gifts to men."
> What does "He ascended" mean except that he also descended into the lower regions of the earth? The one who descended is also the one who ascended far above all the heavens, that he might fill all things (Eph 4:7-10).

This text relates the outpouring of the Spirit, at least insofar as it pertains to the gifts and charisms, to Christ's ascension to heaven. It agrees, therefore, with Luke in linking the outpouring of the Holy Spirit to a precise event that happened after or at the same time as Christ's ascension. In fact, the Acts of the Apostles presents the coming of the Spirit to us in a picture similar to the one in this passage from the Letter to the Ephesians: "Exalted at the right hand of God, he received the promise of the holy Spirit from the Father and poured it forth . . . ." (Acts 2:33).

However, this passage from Ephesians is the only one in the Pauline corpus that links the gift of the Spirit to an "historical" event rather than to a sacramental event, and it is found in a letter whose attribution to St. Paul is not unanimous. Thus, on account of this uncertainty, let us use the expression "Pauline Pentecost" in a wide sense, in the sense, that is, of a certain way that St. Paul has of representing the gift of the Spirit and of relating it to the coming and the work of Jesus.

1. *The Pauline Synthesis on the Holy Spirit*

To this point we have encountered two fundamental conceptions of the Holy Spirit in the New Testament: the charismatic conception of Luke and the other Synoptics that represents the Spirit as a "divine power," particularly as prophecy, and the interior conception of John that represents the Spirit as the principle of rebirth and new life. In St. Paul we find the synthesis of these two lines of thought, not in the sense that he reunites elements that existed separately before him—in fact, he writes before Luke and John—but in the sense that in him both of the perspectives are represented and anticipated.

On the one hand, St. Paul knows *the Spirit as dispenser of the charisms* and as "power of God" and he speaks of it abundantly in his letters (cf. 1 Cor 12–14, Rom 12:6-8, Eph 4:11-16). He knows the "demonstration of spirit and power" (cf. 1 Cor 2:4, 1 Thess 1:5), and he knows it through direct experience from the moment that the Spirit worked "signs and wonders and mighty deeds" (2 Cor 12:12) through him. From this point of view, Paul's novelty with respect to the analogous conception in the Old Testament consists in the fact that now everything is organized around Christ. The charisms come from Christ and are ordained for the edification of his body, the Church. It is he who made some apostles, others evangelists, others prophets (cf. Eph 4:11-12). The novelty also consists in that now "to each individual the manifestation of the Spirit is given for some benefit" (1 Cor 12:7), not only to some privileged members of the people and only on particular occasions as was the case in the Old Testament. St. Paul says that not everyone is an apostle, not everyone performs miracles—in other words, not everyone has every gift (cf. 1 Cor 12:29-30). But everyone has a gift, some in one form, others in another. Unlike Luke, Paul does not limit himself to emphasizing only one charism, prophecy, but stresses many others, although in Paul prophecy also continues to occupy a privileged position (cf. 1 Cor 14:1ff.).

St. Paul is familiar with and gives a great deal of space to the charismatic component of the action of the Holy Spirit, but he is also acquainted with the *Spirit as interior principle of new life,* as constitutive of salvation. The Apostle expresses this new characteristic of the Spirit (scarcely noted in the Old Testament except in a few passages of the prophets on the new covenant, such as Ezek 36:27) in various ways. Let's call to mind the principal ones. The Spirit is the *new law,* the interior law, written in the heart, that founds the new covenant (cf. Rom 7:6, 8:2; 2 Cor 3:6; Titus 3:5). In addition, the Spirit is the principle of a *new knowledge* of God. The faithful have received the Spirit "so that we may understand the things freely given us by God." Even "God's wisdom, mysterious, hidden . . . What eye has not seen, and ear has not heard" God has revealed through the Spirit (cf. 1 Cor 2:7-16). Most important of all, the Spirit is the one who pours *love* into the heart and gives *charity* (cf. Rom 5:5, 1 Cor 12:31–13:1ff.). Finally, for the faithful the Spirit is the *principle of resurrection* and immortality.

All these are different ways of expressing what at bottom is the same truth: that the Spirit not only serves to proclaim salvation but *is* salvation, not only enriches the Church with varied gifts but makes it exist.

2. *Charisms and Charity*

St. Paul knows, therefore, two fundamental actions of the Holy Spirit: the charismatic one that we can define *ad extra,* since it exists for the benefit of everyone and terminates outside the subject who receives it, and the interior one that we can define *ad intra,* since it terminates in the subject who receives it and renews his or her existence. However, Paul does not stop here but also poses explicitly the problem of the mutual relation between these two different operations of the Spirit. His position can be summarized as follows: *recognition of the charisms* as the determining factor for the construction and growth of the body of Christ but *subordination of the charisms to charity,* that is, subordination of the manifestations of the Spirit to his permanent interior dwelling. "Strive eagerly for the greatest spiritual gifts. But I shall show you a still more excellent way" (1 Cor 12:31). With these words St. Paul establishes a double hierarchy: one within the charisms, some of which are "greater" than others, and one between the charisms and charity, the "still more excellent way."

Within the charisms, some, like prophecy, are more beneficial and important than others, such as speaking in tongues: "Strive eagerly for the spiritual gifts, above all that you may prophesy" (1 Cor 14:1ff.) However, within the total work of the Spirit, charity is superior to the charisms, including prophecy, because prophecy will cease whereas charity will never cease (cf. 1 Cor 13:8). "Being" in the Spirit is superior to "acting" (on others) in the Spirit, to such an extent that without charity the rest would be good for nothing.

Why this clear subordination of the charisms to the personal sanctity of the minister? According to the logic of the Gospel, isn't what is to the advantage of others preferable to what is to the advantage of ourselves? Isn't what is of common benefit preferable to what is useful for one alone? St. Augustine explains that the charisms are parts while charity is the whole. "If you love," he says, "you do not have nothing; for if you love unity, whoever in it has anything has it also for you."[1] In the final analysis, love makes one identical with the Giver of the charisms himself, the Holy Spirit, and the Giver is surely preferable to his gifts. For Augustine the Holy Spirit is—not only *naturally* but also *personally*—the love meant when one says "God is love" (1 John 4:8). Infusing love (cf. Rom 5:5), the Holy Spirit does not pour in a thing but himself.[2]

St. Thomas Aquinas also poses the question of why charity (which he calls *gratia gratum faciens,* sanctifying grace) is greater than any charism (which he calls *gratia gratis data,* freely bestowed grace). Notice what he answers. Charity unites directly to the *end,* which is God, whereas the charism only creates the predisposition, prepares the ground, so that he might come into others. It pertains, therefore, to the means, not the end. We ourselves cannot effect *in others* through the charisms what charity effects *in us*—namely, to adhere to God. We can only predispose them to it.[3]

We could deepen St. Thomas' response by saying that charity is also the best and most secure way to act on and assist others. "Love builds up," says the Apostle (1 Cor 8:1) and it also edifies others, builds community, not only ourselves. Moreover, it is indeed charity that preserves the charisms and enables them to work, keeping the person in humble and constant contact with God, the font of the charisms. Without genuine personal sanctity or at least the constant striving towards it through penitence and conversion, the charisms do not resist, are soon corrupted, and easily come to be used for personal glory and benefit instead of "the common good." Jesus himself speaks of charisms that lead to Gehenna because they are not accompanied by doing the will of the Father (cf. Matt 7:21-23).

Nevertheless, we should be careful not to overemphasize this subordination of the charisms to charity, drawing false conclusions from it. Paul speaks by taking into account the situations and needs characteristic of each church. One church—like that in Corinth, which had a strong experience of the charisms and tended to appreciate only the more spectacular manifestations of the Spirit such as speaking in tongues—he forcefully reminds of the importance of charity and says that everything else is nothing without it. But to other churches who did not run this danger and, in fact, ran the opposite danger of being closed to the charisms, as in Thessalonica, the same Apostle urges the contrary: "Do not quench the Spirit" and "Do not despise prophetic utterances" (1 Thess 5:19-20).

It is right to think that Paul would do the same today too. Speaking in environments that experience the charisms directly and powerfully and risk overvaluing them at the expense of a solid life of sanctification, he would say what he said to the Corinthians: "I shall show you a still more excellent way." Speaking instead in environments that tend to look with suspicion on the gifts and charisms and insist only on personal sanctity or the institutional or sacramental action of the Spirit, he would probably say, as he did to the Thessalonians, "Do not quench the Spirit. Do not despise prophetic utterances. Test everything; retain what is good."

3. *The Spirit as "Person"*

With Paul, we do not have only the *synthesis* of the two fundamental actions of the Holy Spirit, one charismatic, the other sanctifying, but we also have the *superseding* of the conception of the Holy Spirit as "action," as "divine power," and as the beginning of the revelation of the Spirit as "person." For St. Paul, the Holy Spirit is not only an *action* but also an *actor,* that is, a principle endowed with will and intelligence who acts consciously and freely. We say of him that he teaches, bears witness, laments, intercedes, grieves, that he knows, that he has desires.

This clear evolution beyond an objective conception of the *Pneuma* towards a personal and subjective one (in which it appears not only as an object but also as a subject, not only an "it" but also a "he") is confirmed by the presence in Paul of triadic formulas like the following: "The grace of the Lord Jesus Christ and the love of God and the fellowship of the holy Spirit be with all of you" (2 Cor 13:13; cf. also 1 Cor 12:4-6, Rom 5:1-5, Gal 4:4-6). Read, as is proper, in the light of Matthew 28:19 ("baptizing them in the name of the Father, and of the Son, and of the holy Spirit") and in light of the later development of the faith, these triadic formulas mark a new orientation towards the Holy Spirit, joined to the revelation concerning the Father and the Son, that is, with the revelation of the Trinity.

One confirmation of this reading comes from John, where the relationship of the Spirit to Jesus Christ is modeled on the relationship of Jesus to the Father. The Father is the one who "testifies" to the Son (cf. John 5:32-37, 8:18) and the Spirit is the one who "testifies" to Jesus (John 15:26). The son does not speak "on his own" but says what he has heard from the Father (John 8:28; 12:49; 14:10). But the Holy Spirit also will not speak "on his own" but will say what he will have heard (John 16:13). Jesus glorifies the Father (John 8:50; 17:1) and the Spirit glorifies Jesus (John 16:14). For John too the Spirit is not only an "it" but also a "he," and perhaps it is for this reason that he puts the masculine name of *Paraclete* beside the neuter name of *Pneuma.*

With that we have hit on a nerve of the Christian faith, and we cannot leave the issue in uncertainty. Whether the Trinity originates from Christ in biblical revelation or, instead, originates outside of the biblical revelation in Hellenistic culture depends on it.

Let's see how the problem is solved in one of the most authoritative syntheses of Biblical pneumatology, the one we find in the *Theological Dictionary of the New Testament,* to which everyone

53

goes back from time to time and from which even I have gotten not a few cues for what I have written so far. "This power," we read concerning the Spirit in St. Paul, "is not anonymous or unknown. It is identical with the exalted Lord once this Lord is considered, not in Himself, but in His work towards the community."[4] The Holy Spirit, therefore, is "identical" to the Risen Lord. But the Pneuma is called by Paul himself the "Spirit of God" and not just the "Spirit of Christ" (cf. 1 Cor 2:10-14; Rom 8). And if the Holy Spirit is identical with the Risen Lord insofar as he acts in the community, how can we ever attribute the resurrection itself to the working of the Spirit (cf. Rom 1:4; 1 Pet 3:18; 1 Tim 3:16)? And what does the phrase "the Spirit of the one who raised Jesus from the dead" mean (Rom 8:11)?

We read further: "The metaphysical question of the relation between God, Christ, and the Spirit is hardly alluded to by Paul at all. For this reason it would be a mistake to think that Paul finds in 'the third person of the Trinity' the original meaning of *Pneuma*. Often *Pneuma* is clearly impersonal. . . ."[5] Now, it is true that in Paul the *Pneuma* often appears as something "impersonal," but it is also true that it just as often appears as something personal, and this is sufficient to say that for him the Spirit already takes form as a personal—that is, free and conscious—reality. How could we deny, for example, the personal character of the Spirit in the following text: "But one and the same Spirit produces all of these, distributing them individually to each person as he wishes" (1 Cor 12:11)? The Spirit is not only the gift or the ensemble of gifts but the free ("as he wishes") distributor who is aware of them.

We conclude that: "it could well be that the question of the personality of the *Pneuma* is wrongly put since neither Hebrew nor Greek has this word."[6] Really, it is this objection itself that is "wrongly put"! Indeed, where does such reasoning lead if consistently applied? It leads us to say that not even the Father and the Son Jesus Christ would be "persons" for Paul because he still lacked such a term and concept. Since the Three are often spoken of together in the same way, what is valid for the Spirit must also be valid for the Father. Therefore, we would need to conclude that the Father too, like the Spirit, is "a way of being" of the Risen Lord, making explicit the Modalism and Monarchianism underlying this reconstruction of New Testament pneumatology.

The absence of a term does not necessarily indicate the absence of the corresponding reality when it is a question of a new reality hitherto unknown. To say the contrary would be the same as saying that the telephone could not have been invented as long as there was no name for it. Is it really the term and its existence that determine the arising of a thing, or is it rather the existence of the thing that determines the rise of the term by which to indicate it? This is valid in a particular way for the concept of the person, or hypostasis, which, inasmuch as it is distinct from "substance," had not existed to that time in any culture and which Christian thought discovered by reflecting on exactly what Jesus had revealed about the Father, the Son, and the Holy Spirit. If you decline to agree to this claim, you cannot explain how and why the term "person" was born.

If person means "to be in relationship"—as even modern thought has finally come to admit, then the personal character of the Holy Spirit in the New Testament is clear because the "relationship" that binds him to the Father and Jesus Christ is clear and distinct. To deny any personal and distinctive character to the *Pneuma,* even in John and in Paul, means inevitably to open the door to the radical conclusion of those theologians who make of the Trinity not the greatest innovation revealed by Christ in the Gospel but the biggest distortion of the Gospel, caused by contact with the Hellenistic world.

We can say then that in St. Paul and in the New Testament there is not yet the term or the concept of personality applied to the Holy Spirit—just as there is not for the Father and not even for Jesus Christ—but there is already the corresponding reality. *Pneuma* is no longer seen as a simple principle or sphere of *action,* as it was in the Hebraic mentality, nor even as a kind of fluid or substance, as in the Greek mindset, but it is seen also as an *agent,* as one who acts distinctly because he speaks of the Son, gives testimony, and is called both Spirit of Christ and Spirit of God. The same principle used to establish the personal distinction between the Father and the Son—"He who begets is one, and he who is begotten is another; he, too, who sends is one, and He who is sent is another"[7]—is also valid for the relations between the Spirit and the Father and the Spirit and the Son—"He who proceeds differs from him who is proceeded from; he who testifies, from the one testified to . . . ."

This does not mean that by applying the concept of person to the Holy Spirit that one has said everything and resolved every problem. As St. Augustine noted, we use the term "person" for lack of a better word, so as not to remain in total silence before God, knowing well, however, that it is inadequate for expressing a reality like the one revealed to us with the names Father, Son, and Holy Spirit.[8]

4. Flesh and Spirit: Two Ways of Being Born, of Living, and of Dying

In his letters the Apostle never expounds the Christian mystery without following up the proclamation with the exhortation to practice, *kerygma* with *paranesis*. In the case of the Holy Spirit, the movement from *kerygma* to *paranesis* and from the gift to the obligation is admirably summed up by the Apostle with these words: "If we live in the Spirit, let us also follow the Spirit" (Gal 5:25). The first verb is in the indicative and it indicates what God has "done" for us; it indicates the gift of the new life in the Spirit or even the "state" in which we find ourselves thanks to baptism. The second verb is a hortatory subjunctive and shows "what is to be done" by us; we are exhorted by it to behave in a manner consistent with what we have become. It is as if the Apostle had said to the Christian: "Be what you have become!" The gift becomes the norm. The Holy Spirit, new life, becomes also the new law for the Christian.

St. Paul makes use of the opposition flesh/Spirit in order to delineate a complete vision of the Christian life—that is, in order to sketch a first draft of theological anthropology. In particular, this opposition serves to explain the three fundamental facts of existence: birth, life, death. In other words, according to the word of God there are two ways to be born—of the flesh and of the Spirit, two ways to live—according to the flesh and according to the Spirit, and two final outcomes—death or eternal life. He says, "The concern of the flesh is death, but the concern of the spirit is life and peace" (Rom 8:6).

First, let us try to clarify the meaning of the two terms flesh and spirit. In everyday usage "flesh" indicates the corporeal component of the human being, referring especially to the sexual sphere, whereas "spirit" indicates reason or the soul, the spiritual component of human beings. In this sense we speak, for example, of the pleasures and sins of the *flesh* or of cultivating one's own *spirit*. This usage has often obscured the genuine biblical meaning of the two terms. In the Bible the opposition flesh/Spirit includes this first meaning, but is not limited to it and is even more radical. Flesh indicates both the body and the soul—the human intelligence and the human will—insofar as they are purely natural realities, marked, moreover, by the experience of sin which makes them inclined to evil. In other words, flesh indicates the whole human being in his precariousness, both physical and moral, inasmuch as he is infinitely distant from God who is Spirit (cf. John 4:24). To use a modern expression, flesh indicates the "human condition." To say that the "Word was made flesh" (cf. John 1:14) is to say it was made human, that it assumed the human condition. What, then, does the word "Spirit" mean? It means divine reality, grace, and everything that a human being is and does when moved by this new and superior principle. In the opposition flesh/Spirit, Spirit always indicates, directly or indirectly, the Holy Spirit and hence should be written with a capital letter.

In order to get an idea of the difference between the current and the biblical usage of these terms, it is enough to say that the act commonly held to be the most "carnal" of all can be, in the biblical vision, an exquisitely spiritual act, a deed according to the Spirit, if it is performed in the bosom of matrimony with love and in reverence for the will of the Creator. Whereas the act considered the most spiritual of all—to philosophize—judged by the Bible's yardstick is a work of the flesh, if one does it following a logic of egoism to exalt himself or his own race or if through it error and lies are taught. In fact, St. Paul calls all that "concern of the flesh" (Rom 8:7). Besides, we know that what we normally mean by the word "spirit"—when we speak of the "spirit of the times" or the "spirit of the world"—is exactly what the Bible would call "flesh."

Thus, in the biblical opposition flesh/Spirit, not only is the opposition between instinct and reason or between body and soul at stake but also the more radical opposition between nature and grace, the human and the divine, the terrestrial and the eternal, egoism and love. Flesh and Spirit indicate two worlds or two different spheres of action. Having clarified the difference between these terms, we can now illustrate the affirmation made above that for the Bible there are two ways of being born (from the flesh and from the Spirit), two ways of living (according to the flesh and according to the Spirit), and two ways of concluding life (either with death or with eternal life).

Two ways of being born. The Bible designates the natural birth from father and mother in different ways. It calls it birth "of flesh" (John 3:6), "by natural generation . . . by human choice . . . [or] by a man's decision" (John 1:13), "from perishable . . . seed" (1 Pet 1:23). We should pay heed not to see here any negative judgment or condemnation of human generation and birth in themselves. The Bible knows that, in the final analysis, natural birth too is from God, who created humans male and female exactly so that they would become fruitful and fill the earth. To come into the world is a gift and not a prison sentence, as in antiquity the Platonists and Gnostics thought.

If there is a negative connotation in these expressions, it is not so much due to what human birth is in itself as much as to what it is not, not so much to what it possesses as to what it still lacks. The best proof of this is that even Jesus is said to have been born "descended from David according to the flesh" (Rom 1:3). Not even the belief in original sin annuls the fundamentally positive value of human life and thus of natural birth. Moreover, in the biblical sources original sin is never so narrowly tied to the mode of transmission of life through sexual generation as it will be later from Augustine on down.

And we come to the *birth according to the Spirit.* The birth of the Spirit is also designated with diverse expressions: "of God" (John 1:13), "from above" (John 3:3), "from imperishable seed, through the living and abiding word of God" (1 Peter 1:23). This birth, or rebirth, happens at the initiative and will of God the Father who brings it about through the Spirit. The life that results from this new birth is life "in Christ" or life "in the Spirit." The "seed" by which this new life is transmitted is the word of God, received through faith.

The new birth is always connected with faith: "Everyone who believes that Jesus is the Christ is begotten by God" (1 John 5:1).

The same thing is said, several times, in other ways. In reality, it is not we who are born anew but it is Christ who is conceived and born in us "through the working of the Holy Spirit." But it's the same thing, seen from different angles. Since all this is concretely made real in baptism, the new birth is said to be "of water and Spirit" (John 3:5). Whoever passes through this experience, this initiation, is called a "new creature," and just as through natural birth one becomes a child of man, a child of a father and a mother, whoever goes through this rebirth becomes a child of God (cf. Rom 8:14, 1 John 3:1).

Two ways of living. In continuity with these two types of birth—of the flesh and of the Spirit—the Bible also speaks of two different ways or styles of life that define, respectively, life according to the flesh and life according to the Spirit. St. Paul describes them almost in the style of the "parallel lives" [of Plutarch]: "For those who live according to the flesh are concerned with the things of the flesh, but those who live according to the Spirit with the things of the Spirit. The concern of the flesh is death, but the concern of the Spirit is life and peace. For the concern of the flesh is hostility towards God; it does not submit to the law of God nor can it; and those who are in the flesh cannot please God" (Rom 8:5-8).

To live according to the flesh means to live on a natural level without faith. Those who live according to the flesh live according to nature—not original nature, the one created good and straight by God that still makes its voice heard, however weakened, through the conscience, but nature corrupted by sin which expresses itself by means of the various desires and above all through egoism. The typical manifestations of a life set up in this way are the so-called "works of the flesh": "immorality, impurity, licentiousness, idolatry, sorcery, hatreds, rivalry, jealousy, outbursts of fury, acts of selfishness, dissensions, factions, occasions of envy, drinking bouts, orgies, and the like" (Gal 5:19-20).

In contrast, *to live according to the Spirit* means to think, will, and act moved within by that principle of new life placed in us at baptism, which is the Spirit of Jesus. To live according to the Spirit is equivalent, therefore, to imitating Christ. The manifestations characteristic of this new life are the so-called "fruits of the

Spirit": "love, joy, peace, patience, kindness, generosity, faithfulness, gentleness, self-control" (Gal 5:22).

Two ways to die. And we come finally to the two different outcomes to which living according to the flesh and living according to the Spirit, respectively, lead: death or life. "For if you live according to the flesh, you will die, but if by the spirit you put to death the deeds of the body, you will live" (Rom 8:13). If someone lives according to the flesh, in a purely natural and earthly perspective, since the "flesh" is by definition that which passes away, is corrupted, has a beginning, a period of development, and an end, the ultimate horizon of such a life can only be death. All flesh, the Bible says, is like grass and "the flower of the field. / The grass withers, the flower wilts . . . ." (Isa 40:6-7). From this point of view, the philosopher who defined human being as "Being-towards-death" is perfectly right.⁹ As soon as one is born, one begins to die. One cannot go beyond this horizon: the human being is born and lives in order to die.

But if someone lives according to the Spirit, since the Spirit is, by definition, that which does not decay, the eternal, the horizon in this case does not close with death. The new life of the Spirit has a beginning but not an end: "the one who sows for his flesh will reap corruption from the flesh, but the one who sows for the spirit will reap eternal life from the spirit" (Gal 6:8).

Seen in this "spiritual" perspective, the human being no long seems a "being-towards-death" but rather a being-towards-eternity! Truly, not even the flesh will finish forever in corruption thanks to the resurrection of the dead. But this—to give back life even to our body at the end of time—will be precisely the ultimate great work of the Spirit: "If the Spirit of the one who raised Jesus from the dead dwells in you, the one who raised Christ from the dead will give life to your mortal bodies also, through his Spirit that dwells in you" (Rom 8:11).

NOTES

1. St. Augustine, *Tractates on the Gospel of John 28–54,* vol. 3, *The Fathers of the Church,* vol. 78, trans. John W. Rettig (Washington, D.C.: The Catholic University Press, 1993) 48. [32.8]

2. See St. Augustine, *The Trinity*, trans. Stephen McKenna, C.S.S.R., *The Fathers of the Church*, vol 45., (Washington, D.C.: The Catholic University Press, 1963) 495–6. [15.17.31]

3. See St. Thomas Aquinas, *Summa Theologiae*, vol. 30, trans. Cornelius Ernst, O.P. (London: Blackfriars, 1972) 141–3. [I-IIae, q.111, a.5]

4. Eduard Schweizer, in the *Theological Dictionary of the New Testament*, vol. 6, ed. Gerhard Friedrich, trans. Geoffrey Bromiley (Grand Rapids, Mich.: Eerdmans, 1968) 433.

5. Ibid.

6. Ibid., 433–4.

7. Tertullian, "Against Praxeas," *The Anti-Nicene Fathers*, vol. 3, ed. Roberts and Donaldson (New York: Scribner's, 1925) 604. [9.2]

8. See St. Augustine, *The Trinity*, 236ff. [7.6.11]

9. Martin Heidegger, *Being and Time*, trans. Macquarrie and Robinson (New York: Harper and Row, 1962) 296ff.